The
Changing Shape of
CHURCH HISTORY

The
Changing Shape of
CHURCH HISTORY

Justo L. González

CHALICE™
PRESS
ST. LOUIS, MISSOURI

Biblical quotations, unless otherwise noted, are from the *New Revised Standard Version Bible*, copyright 1989, Division of Christian Education of the National Council of the Churches of Christ in the United States of America. Used by permission. All rights reserved.

Cover art: © PhotoDisc, Inc
Cover and interior design: Elizabeth Wright
Art direction: Elizabeth Wright

This book is printed on acid-free, recycled paper.

Visit Chalice Press on the World Wide Web at
www.chalicepress.com

10 9 8 7 6 5 4 3 2 1   02 03 04 05 06 07

Library of Congress Cataloging-in-Publication Data

González, Justo L.
  The changing shape of church history / Justo L. González.
      p. cm.
Includes bibliographical references.
  ISBN 0-8272-0490-6 (alk. paper)
  1. Church history–Historiography. 2. Developing countries–Church history–Historiography. I. Title.
  BR138 .G66 2002
  270'.7'2–dc21

                                                2002007782

Printed in the United States of America

Contents

Preface   vii

Introduction   1

Part I: The Changing Geography of Church History

1. The Changing Cartography   7
2. The Changing Topography   19
3. Cataclysmic Changes   33
4. The Failing Map of Modernity   47
5. Mapping a New Catholicity   63

Part II: The Changing History of Church History

6. The Struggle over the History of Israel   83
7. The Struggle over Greco-Roman History   99
8. The Struggle over Secular History   115
9. The Struggle over the History of the Church   131
10. The Future of Church History   145

Notes   155

Preface

The materials that comprise this book were developed as lectures delivered at various academic institutions. Most of the material included in this book is based on lectures delivered at McCormick Theological Seminary (the Zenos Lecture Series), at Golden Gate Baptist Theological Seminary (the Deere Lectures), at Seabury-Western Theological Seminary (the Stewart Lectures), and at Western Theological Seminary (the Osterhaven Lectures). They were prepared as the second millennium drew to a close, and edited and reorganized early in the third millennium. They were also translated and adapted for delivery in Spanish at the Baptist Seminary in Santiago, Chile, under the sponsorship of ASIT, the regional association of theological schools. The rest of the material is based on lectures delivered originally in Spanish in Buenos Aires, at the Baptist Seminary and at the Instituto Superior de Estudios Teológicos (ISEDET), also under the sponsorship of ASIT.

The beginning of the third millennium is an appropriate time for taking stock of the manner in which the life of the church is developing, how this is affecting the discipline of church history, and what historical resources the church has for facing the issues of the coming decades. That is the purpose of the chapters that follow.

A preface is an opportunity to express gratitude. I therefore take this occasion to thank the institutions named above, as well as their administration, faculty, and students, for the kind reception of the lectures delivered there, for their warm hospitality, and especially for the many points in which dialogue with them enriched and improved what I brought to their respective schools.

Special thanks also to Bonnie Shoemaker, who saved me many hours of work by her careful and enthusiastic transcription support.

Introduction

Where is the cutting edge of church history? Is it in some of the very interesting books that have been published recently on the relationship between pagan and Christian in the early centuries of the life of the church? Is it in the analysis of the wealth of material on gnosticism that has appeared in the last few decades? Is it in the many medieval manuscripts that are being published every year? Is it in the study of hitherto almost unknown medieval mystics and heretics? Is it in the new interpretations of Luther, Calvin, Wesley, or some of the other towering figures of church history? Is it in the many dissertations that are being written every year in universities throughout the world, many of them on topics so arcane that it is no wonder that no one has studied them before? Clearly, depending on your own interests, and even on your likes and dislikes, any of these could be considered the cutting edge of church history.

Even more importantly for the life of the church today, how is that cutting edge related to ministry? As one considers the multiplicity of possible cutting edges, and the somewhat esoteric nature of some of them, the task of relating them to ministry in the twenty-first century becomes ever more daunting.

Perhaps what makes this question so difficult to answer is that we are looking at it with a microscope when it would be best to look at it with a wide-angle lens. Perhaps the cutting edge of church history is not in some detailed study of a particular moment of church history. That may well be part of the cutting edge. But the cutting edge is much larger than that. The cutting edge is really in the new and unforeseen directions that church history is now taking.

1

As I survey the field of church history at the beginning of the third millennium, I am struck by the sweeping changes that have taken place since I first began working in the field, and which are still taking place at an ever increasing speed. In a word, the entire field of church history is changing, to the point that church history today is no longer what it was thirty years ago, and we only have an inkling of what it will be thirty years from now.

At this point someone may ask, how is it possible for the past to change? Obviously, it is not possible. But history is not the same as the past. The past is never directly accessible to us. The past comes to us through the mediation of interpretation. And that interpreted past is history.

Perhaps a good way to put it is using the image of a dialogue. In a dialogue, the other is not directly accessible to me. All that I have are words, gestures, and tones by which the other person attempts to communicate with me, but which I receive and interpret according to my own experiences and presuppositions. In a genuine dialogue, I must respect the otherness of my interlocutor. I must not interpret the other's words according to my own whims. There is a givenness to those words. On the other hand, no matter how hard I try, the only way in which I can hear and interpret those words is from my own perspective. When you stop to think about it, dialogue is impossible. And yet, in spite of its impossibility, it happens! Pure, unhindered communication is but an elusive dream. And yet communication is the basis of all social life. I know as I write these lines that not one of my readers will understand my words exactly as I mean them—in fact, no two of them will understand them in exactly the same way. And yet I persist in writing. That is the miracle of communication, which, although impossible, is still the fabric of all social life.

Now think about history as a dialogue. It is a dialogue in which it is not only the past that addresses us, but also we who address the past. As a historian, I am not a passive observer of past events, but an interlocutor who speaks with the past, who poses questions to the past. And the answers the past gives me depend to a large measure on the questions I ask of it.

What all this means is that the changes that are taking place in church history are the counterpart of the changes that are taking place in the church today.

It is this that makes history so pertinent for today–not that it is what happened in the past, but rather that it is what happened in the past as seen from our present and toward the future we imagine.

The history of the church is changing, not just because scholars have new sources, but even more so because the church and the world are changing. And these are changes that we can only begin to understand as we look at them in historical perspective.

The third millennium had barely begun when the world was shaken by an act of terrorism apparently without precedent. In a few hours, the previously "friendly skies" had rained death upon thousands in the United States. As a few months have passed and we have had time to reflect on the matter, we are coming to the realization that what was unprecedented in the events of September 11, 2001, was not the toll in lives destroyed–indeed, it would be possible to cite several events, even in recent history, in which more lives were lost. Nor is it true to say that the unprecedented part of this particular case was the loss of civilian life. For the last three hundred years, the level of civilian casualties has been constantly rising as war has followed war; and, likewise, there have been numerous events–for instance, in Cambodia and in Rwanda–in which the number of civilian deaths has risen into the hundreds of thousands, and even the millions. What is clearly unprecedented in the events of September 11 is that they revealed the vulnerability of all humankind–even those who could otherwise consider themselves most invulnerable. September 11 united peoples and nations in a sense not only of loss but also and above all of vulnerability, and this is probably one of the reasons why it was relatively easy to form a wide coalition of nations committed to put a stop to terrorism–or at least to the groups most directly connected with this particular act, for exactly what "terrorism" is depends on one's definition.

At any rate, the events of September 11 will mark the manner in which church history–as well as all human history–is written in the present generation. September 11 is a clear confirmation that, as we shall see in the chapters that follow, the map of the world is changing–not just that borders are being redefined and new nations are being born, but even more that the centers of power, and even the very nature of power, are shifting. September 11 has made us acutely aware that the world is not really as secular as Western modernity had thought, that many nations are no longer culturally or religiously homogeneous, that events in the past that many of us did not consider important still have great power to shape the future.

All these changes, which will soon become apparent in the writing of world history, are also impacting the history of Christianity. In a word, church history will no longer be what it used to be. The purpose of the chapters that follow is to attempt to outline some of the most likely and significant changes that have already begun to take place in the field of church history and that are likely to have a lasting impact on the field.

PART I

The Changing Geography of Church History

1

The Changing Cartography

History and Geography

As a central image for describing and discussing the changes that are taking place in church history, I have decided to use the metaphor of geography. However, in a way this is more than a metaphor, for there is indeed a connection between history and geography. If history is a drama, then geography is the stage on which the action flows. No matter how much one focuses on the plot, it is impossible to understand or to follow the action without its setting on the stage. Indeed, much of the plot has to do with the placing of the various actors on the stage, with their entering and exiting, with the various props that establish the setting, with the movement of the actors up- or downstage. Likewise, I learned many years ago that it is impossible to follow history without an understanding of the stage on which it takes place.

I must confess that in my own academic career, in my early years of study, the subject that I most disliked was history. Then I realized that one of the reasons I disliked it was because I was trying to understand events only in their chronological sequence, as if the geography or the stage on which they took place were unimportant. Thus, what ought to have been the fascinating study of people's lives became a series of names and dates hanging in mid-air, of disembodied ghosts parading through my textbooks in rapid and confusing succession. It was only when I began seeing them as actual people with their feet on the ground, and when I began understanding the movements of peoples and nations not only across time and chronology but also across space and geography, that history became fascinating to me.

As a professor, I have become convinced that one of the main obstacles in the teaching and the learning of church history is that the geography in which that history takes place is alien and unknown to most students. I may be fascinated with the theological and hermeneutical contrasts between Alexandria and Antioch, and spend an hour explaining those contrasts and their consequences for christology or for soteriology, only to find at the end of the hour that many of my students do not have the faintest idea where to place Alexandria or Antioch on a map of the Roman Empire.

My wife also teaches church history. Some years ago she began to suspect that one of the reasons why some students had enormous difficulties understanding the history of the ancient and medieval church was that they lacked even a basic understanding of geography. One year, at the very first class, before saying even the first word about history, she handed out blank maps of Europe and the Roman Empire and asked the students to locate on those maps a list of cities and places. Almost all knew enough geography to place Rome somewhere in the boot of Italy. Most knew that Jerusalem was somewhere toward the eastern edge of the Mediterranean. But there their knowledge ended. One student put Ireland in the Ukraine. Another moved Spain to Germany, and Egypt to Spain. Alexandria drifted all the way from Egypt to Great Britain, and the unfortunate Libyans were freezing north of Moscow. Only one student out of a class of about fifty college graduates knew enough European geography to be able to place correctly the list of twenty names they were given—and that student was a Korean!

Needless to say, since then one of the required textbooks for that introductory course on church history is a good historical atlas.

Having had our laugh at beginning students of theology, it is time that we historians and professors of theology look at the beams in our own eyes. True, we know more or less where to place Alexandria on the map, and we would never place Spain east of the Rhine, but are we sufficiently aware of the manner in which the map of the church has changed during our own lifetimes, and the manner in which that is beginning to affect the reading and the writing of church history?

The changes in the map of Christianity should be evident to anyone who is aware of the manner in which Christianity has evolved during the last few decades. At the beginning of the twentieth century, half of all Christians in the world lived in Europe. Now that figure is less than a quarter. At the beginning of that century, approximately four out of five Christians were white. At the end of the century, less than two out of five. At the beginning of the century, the great missionary centers of Christianity were New York and London. Today more missionaries are sent from Korea than from London, and Puerto Rico is sending missionaries to New York by the dozen. A hundred years ago, there were less than 10 million Christians in Africa, less than 22 million in Asia, and some 5 million in Oceania; now those numbers have risen to 360 million, 312 million, and 22 million respectively. Meanwhile, growth in the North Atlantic has been much less spectacular (from 460 to 821 million), and in most cases has not kept up with population growth.[1]

The Old Map

What this means is that the map of Christianity on which we operated a few decades ago is no longer operational. That was a map in which the center was the North Atlantic—Europe and North America. Apart from a few churches whose interest was mostly as relics of an ancient past, there was little outside the North Atlantic to attract the attention of historians. And these historians themselves were either persons from the North Atlantic, or persons who, as myself, had been trained into the North Atlantic reading of history.

A few examples should suffice to make this point.

First, a look at the basic textbook on church history on which most of my generation was formed. That was Williston

Walker's *A History of the Christian Church*. Although by the time I went to seminary this book had gone through a number of revisions, its basic outline was the same as that of the original edition. Most of my comments are based on the 1959 edition, revised by Cyril C. Richardson, Wilhelm Pauck, and Robert T. Handy, which was published just as I was preparing for my doctoral exams at Yale.[2]

It appears that the main criterion of the selection process in Walker's *History* is the importance of various events and developments for North American Protestant self-understanding. Indeed, the table of contents is such that many a North American Protestant will be able to read most of the book and say, "this is my story." The narrative is almost exclusively limited to the Roman Empire in the early centuries, then to Western Europe, and after the Reformation to the North Atlantic. The conversion of Armenia is mentioned almost parenthetically in a sentence dealing with the spread of Monophysism. The church in Ethiopia ranks a bit more space—about half a paragraph, again in a section dealing with the Monophysite revolt resulting from Justinian's policies. The spread of Islam also merits half a paragraph—a paragraph that also deals with the Lombards, the Avars, the Croats, the Serbs, and several others. Another paragraph takes care of the Spanish *Reconquista*. The significance of Arabic civilization for the theological renaissance of the twelfth and thirteenth centuries, and in particular for the development of Thomism, is barely mentioned. The crucial role of Sicily and Spain in that encounter between civilizations is not mentioned at all.

Then comes the Reformation of the sixteenth century. The period is covered in 121 pages, of which slightly less than seven are devoted to Roman Catholicism. In that brief section on Catholicism, attention is paid to monastic and mystical movements, to anti-Protestant polemics, and to the Council of Trent. But not a word is said about the very active theological work that was taking place in the Roman Catholic Church quite apart from any anti-Protestant concern. Those seven pages also include a passing reference to Ricci in China and De Nobili in India. Francis Suárez, foundational theologian for the Jesuit order, is conspicuously absent. The story of Roman Catholicism is picked up in another nine pages toward the end of the book, dealing with "Modern Roman Catholicism," which covers the entire development from Jansenism to the time the book was written.

After the Iconoclastic controversy, the Eastern churches receive two pages for the rest of their medieval development, and then a final chapter of seven pages to bring their story up to date.

This may sound quite critical, and indeed it is. Yet it must be pointed out that as a seminary student the only place in the theological curriculum, apart from a belated course on ecumenism, where I had even an inkling of the existence of Christians and churches in Ethiopia or in Armenia was through this book and others like it.

A New Consciousness Requires a New Map

Still, when I review the manner in which I first studied church history, and the cartography that lay behind that history as an unspoken presupposition, I am surprised and dismayed at the degree to which I allowed that telling of the narrative to become part of my story, even though in many ways it marginalized me and my community.

Walker's book, as well as all the others that were used as textbooks at the time, tended to reduce the significance of the sixteenth century to the Protestant Reformation and its Roman Catholic counterpart. That was understandable. These were mostly Protestant books, written at a time when there was still great alienation between Protestants and Catholics, and they were also books from the North Atlantic, written from a perspective in which the North Atlantic was the new *mare nostrum* of the new imperial civilization. Significantly, even though I had studied the history of the conquest and colonization of the Western Hemisphere ever since I was in the second grade, as I read those books in seminary it did not occur to me that there was a great omission. Today, I cannot speak of the history of the church in the sixteenth century without taking into account that on May 26, 1521, the same day that the Imperial Diet of Worms issued its edict against Luther, Hernán Cortés was laying siege to the imperial city of Tenochtitlán. And today, after the Second Vatican Council and a number of developments in Latin America, many would agree that the jury is still out as to which of those two events will eventually prove to be more important for the history of the church at large—a point to which I shall return in chapter 3.

Today I must work with a different set of maps. Indeed, today I must work with a map that no longer places the North Atlantic at the center, but is, rather, a polycentric map. This is perhaps the most radical change that has taken place in the cartography of church history. In the past, we could speak of a center, or at most of two centers, and tell the story from those centers outward. Today that is no longer possible. Today there are many centers, both in the actual life of the church and in the way the past history of the church is being written.

A Polycentric Map

It may be helpful to stop and think about the polycentric nature of today's Christianity. To a degree without parallel in the history of the church, today the centers of vitality are not the same as the centers of economic resources. And those centers are more than one. In times past, there have been many changes in the geography of Christianity. Already in the New Testament, we see the center shifting from Jerusalem to Antioch and even toward Asia Minor. Yet it is also clear that at that time, as the importance of the church in Jerusalem wanes in comparison with the rest of Christianity, so also do its economic resources wane, so that a significant part of Paul's mission is to collect funds for the saints in Jerusalem.

When the Empire becomes Christian, the center of Christianity once again shifts, this time to the centers of political power. At first, this is Constantinople, and therefore one should not be surprised that all the early ecumenical councils of the Christian church take place in Constantinople or nearby—Nicea, Ephesus, Chalcedon.

Later, when the Islamic invasions and the Carolingian renaissance shift the center to Western Europe, it is clear that there is a new center, not only in vitality, but also in political power and even in the relatively meager economic resources of the time. Henri Pirenne has stated this quite starkly:

> The West was blockaded and forced to live upon its own resources. For the first time in history the axis of life was

shifted northwards from the Mediterranean. The decadence into which the Merovingian monarchy lapsed as a result of this change gave birth to a new dynasty, the Carolingian, whose original home was in the Germanic North.

With this new dynasty the Pope allied himself, breaking with the Emperor [in Constantinople]...And so the Church allied itself with the new order of things. In Rome, and in the Empire which it founded, it had no rival.[3]

Thus, if until that time the center of Christianity was along an East-West axis along the Mediterranean basin, after that time the center was along a North-South axis that would eventually run from the British Isles, through France, and on to Rome—with a smaller, independent center in Constantinople.

The "discoveries" and colonial expansion of Western Europe, which had their beginnings in the late fifteenth century but reached their high point in the colonial and missionary enterprises of the nineteenth and early twentieth centuries, once again shifted the center of Christianity, which now was the North Atlantic. The theological, missionary, and economic center was in Western Europe—particularly Northwestern Europe—and North America. Out of that center, Western European colonial, economic, and religious power expanded to the rest of the world. Kenneth Scott Latourette has stated the new situation quite bluntly:

By A.D. 1914 all the land surface of the world was politically subject to European peoples except a few spots in Africa, some of the Asiatic states, Japan, a little corner of Southeastern Europe, and the jungles in the interior of some of the largest of the islands of the Pacific. Even the lands which had not submitted politically had been touched by the commerce of Europeans and most of them had been modified by European culture.[4]

He then relates that colonial, economic, and technological expansion to the advance of Christianity:

The fact that the emerging world culture had its origins in the Occident was of advantage to Christianity. Because of the Western source of that culture and because Christianity was traditionally the religion of the West, the way was opened for the Christian impulse to become a constituent part of that culture and to help shape it.[5]

These past shifts of the centers of Christianity—from Jerusalem, to Antioch, to Constantinople, to Western Europe, to the North Atlantic—should lead us to expect similar shifts, so that the changes that have taken place in the late twentieth and early twenty-first centuries should not surprise us. Already by the time Latourette completed his monumental seven-volume *History of the Expansion of Christianity* he was well aware of the demise of colonialism and of the potentially negative consequences of the situation he had described earlier. He was also aware that the center of Christianity was beginning to shift, as the traditionally Christian West became more secular, and churches elsewhere gained in vitality.

However, the change that was taking place was different from the previous changes in the centers of Christianity. In the previous cases—from Jerusalem to Antioch, to Constantinople, and so forth— a shift in the center of power had also implied a shift in the center of numbers, finances, vitality, creativity, and so on.

Today the situation is quite different. There is no doubt that the vast majority of the financial resources of the church are still in the North Atlantic. Indeed, the budget of some of our major seminaries in the United States is larger than the total budget of many a denomination overseas. And some congregations in the United States own buildings that are worth more than all the holdings of entire denominations elsewhere. The same is true of the number of magazines and books published, resources invested in the media, and so on. And yet, proportionately speaking, the number of Christians in the North Atlantic continues to dwindle, while there is an explosion in church membership in traditionally poorer countries.

That is the first dimension of what I mean by affirming that the emerging geography of Christianity is polycentric. From the point of view of resources, the centers are still in the United States, Canada, and Western Europe. From the point of view of vitality, missionary and evangelistic zeal, and even theological creativity, the centers have been shifting south for some time.

The second dimension of the new polycentric reality is that even in the South there is no new center. Exciting new theological insights are coming from Peru as well as from South Africa and the Philippines. Phenomenal growth is happening in Chile as well as in Brazil, Uganda, and Korea. No single place can now be called *the* center of Christianity, nor even one of the few centers.

Consequences of the New Map

This new map of Christianity in turn implies a different reading of church history, at least on two points.

The first of these is that it is no longer possible to separate the history of the church from the history of missions or the history of the expansion of Christianity. The manner in which church history has been traditionally read, written, and taught—not only in the North Atlantic, but even throughout the world—made it appear that North Atlantic Christianity was the goal of church history, and that therefore, everything that did not lead to it was part of a different field of study, usually called the "history of missions" or some other similar name. Thus, the conversion of the Roman Empire and the conversion of the Germanic tribes were part of church history, but the conversion of Ethiopia and the planting of Christianity in Japan were part of the history of missions. The controversy over the presence of Christ in the eucharist during the Carolingian period was part of church history, but the controversy over the Chinese rites in the Roman Catholic Church was not. The debates over the veneration of images in eighth-century Europe were part of church history, but the debate over the veneration of ancestors in nineteenth-century Asia was not.

Such distinctions are no longer possible. Since the new map of Christianity does not have the North Atlantic at the center, the new outline of church history no longer has North Atlantic Christendom as the point of view from which to look at the past. Precisely because Christianity has become polycentric, church history has become global and ecumenical in a way that would have been inconceivable a few generations ago.

This leads to the second point at which the new map of the church requires a different reading of church history. When I first studied church history, it was taken for granted that the essence of Christianity was fairly well determined by the fourth century. It was generally acknowledged that Christianity as we have come to know it was the result of the encounter between the original Palestinian movement and the dominant Greco-Roman culture of the time. Although Adolf von Harnack and other historians had raised questions as to whether this represented a betrayal of the original impulse of Christianity, in general this adaptation of the faith to the dominant culture of the Hellenistic world was considered unavoidable and, by the more orthodox church historians, generally positive. After that time, however, Christianity was expected to remain essentially the same, perhaps with some minor variations in emphasis. Thus, the conversion of the Germanic people was examined in terms of their being added to the church, with very little consideration given to the degree to which that addition brought with itself new and different understandings of the faith. After all, most of those doing church history considered themselves the intellectual, spiritual, and even genetic heirs to Christianity, Greco-Roman civilization, and Germanic invaders all bundled into one. All these were part of the mainstream leading to North Atlantic Christianity, and therefore, although the differences among them were acknowledged, they were not considered to be such that the three could not be joined into a single Christianity.

It is all of this that contributed to the earlier map of church history, in which the center had been formed by the commingling of early Christianity first with Greco-Roman civilization and then with Germanic traditions. Beyond that center, everything else was periphery, valid only to the degree to which it reflected the values and the understandings of the center—a periphery to which the center had the obligation to bring its benefits, its superior understanding, its purer faith.

The map of the church has changed repeatedly through the centuries. From a sect limited to Palestine and its surrounding region, it soon spread throughout the Roman Empire and beyond. By the fourth century, the map had come to include Ethiopia, Armenia, Georgia, Persia, and perhaps even India. By the eighth, China was part of the map. Then came the age of the great expansion of the European powers, and the map changed even more radically, rapidly including Africa, Asia, the entire Western Hemisphere; then Australia, New Zealand, and the islands of the Pacific.

But although these changes have taken place in the map of Christianity in purely geographic terms, in ideological terms the map has remained the same since the times of Eusebius–to whom I shall return in chapter 7. The way Eusebius tells the history of the church, God's plan was not only that Jewish revelation and Greco-Roman culture would come together in Christianity, but also that Christianity and the Empire should come together in Constantine.

Ever since that time, while the map has been expanding, its ideological structure has not changed. It is a bigger map, but it has usually remained a monocentric and providential map, one in which the historian stands at the apex and looks back at history as somehow culminating in the present–and specifically in the historian's present. What cannot be seen as part of that movement has little or no place in the narrative of history, and must at best be seen as a matter of condescension, a white man's burden, a responsibility that it is the duty of the historian's community to discharge in a sort of noblesse oblige.

The new map is very different. As Christianity has become a truly universal religion, with deep roots in every culture, it is also becoming more and more contextualized, and therefore, out of its many centers come different readings of the entire history of the church. The result is frightening and exhilarating.

I find it frightening because in many ways it means that I constantly have to relearn much of my own discipline. I can no longer read the past out of a single perspective or out of a single context. I must somehow listen to those voices from other centers and from the margins that speak from different perspectives and see a past that is not exactly the same as I have seen. In fact, I can no longer speak of a single past, for out of these many centers and many perspectives come many pasts. Sometimes the chaos is such that one even fears that the entire discipline of church history might explode into a thousand fragments, and no one will be able to put it together again.

On the other hand, this is an exhilarating time in which to be doing church history, for it clearly shows that church history is not already done. The very fluidity of our maps, and the ensuing fluidity of the past, mean that we have the freedom and the necessity to write church history all over again. Each time I read what I have written on church history, I wish I could write it all over again, for the story is not quite right; there is still another insight from another perspective that must be taken into account.

My brother's field of study was the Hebrew Bible. Once my mother quipped that she wished at least one of her two sons had decided to deal with someone or with something that was still alive. Were she to say that to me today, I would answer that church history is very much alive, that it is changing, that it is growing, that it is fun! And all that because the map of church history is changing so drastically.

2

The Changing Topography

Chapter 1 explored how the geography of church history is changing in the sense that the map itself is being transformed. This means not only that the map has become larger as the church has become a global reality, but even more that it is no longer possible to write the history of the church as Eusebius wrote it, and as most of his successors wrote it, with the historian standing at what appears to be the center of Christianity and the culmination of past history. The postmodern polycentric map of Christianity will no longer allow that.[1]

But geography is not concerned only with the horizontal expanse of the land. It is also concerned with the vertical, with the mountains and the valleys, or in other words, with the topography of the land. Indeed, geography reduced to a flat map falsifies reality, as anyone who has compared the projections of Mercator, Goode, and Peeters has discovered. Every such projection inevitably errs by distorting reality in one direction or another. Likewise, any flat map has to be corrected in order to take topography into account. And in this sense also the geography of church history is undergoing drastic changes.

New Voices

Allow me to illustrate those changes with a personal note. When I first studied church history, in a seminary in Latin America, all our textbooks either were written in English or were Spanish translations of books originally written in English. I stated above that my generation was formed on Williston Walker's book. But in fact my very first textbook on church history was Kenneth Scott Latourette's *A History of Christianity.*[2] At that point there was no Spanish translation of that book, and most of my classmates knew very little English. It was also the time before computers and even photocopy machines. So every evening the entire class would gather. There were seventeen of us in the class. I would translate the book out loud, while four typists wrote down what I said, making four copies each, and the rest of the class would proofread and collate what was being produced. I remember telling one of my professors after one of those sessions, "someone should write a textbook on church history in Spanish, one that deals more with our issues and concerns." He had some experience in the publishing world and said, "That will never be possible. The market is not large enough."

That was a little over forty years ago. In those four decades, which from the point of view of world history are little more than an instant, things have changed drastically. The book of which I spoke, and that my professor very wisely considered impossible, has been written, as have many others that would have been considered unpublishable a few generations ago. The church in Latin America has grown enough so that the market can now support such books. But even more, the book that I had vaguely hoped to write, and that my professor had discouraged, has been translated into English and several other languages, and now there are not only Latin American students, but also North American white students, Korean students, and Chinese students who are using that book as a textbook, and whose first readings in church history are therefore from a book written from a Latino perspective.

That small personal experience, multiplied a hundredfold, illustrates the first point at which the topography of church history, and the topography of the church itself, are changing. More and more, voices previously unheard are being heard. This includes people of color in the white-dominated North Atlantic, women both in the North Atlantic and elsewhere, and people in what we used to call the Third World or the "younger churches." (At this point, allow me to make a comment about my use of the phrase "the Third World." With good reason, some prefer to speak of "the Two-Thirds World," thus indicating that what we used to call "the Third World" is much more than all the rest put together. I prefer to speak of "the Third World" in a sense similar to that in which Constantinople began calling itself "the Second Rome," and Moscow "the Third Rome." Thus, the phrase "the Third World" is used to suggest the possibility that this may indeed be the world of the future, after the hegemonies of the other two have passed. It was in this sense, as an alternative to both the capitalist West and the socialist East, that the Bandung Conference first employed this term.)

New Questions

All these people, myself included, are asking of the past different questions than most church historians were asking fifty years ago. The result is an unparalleled change in the topography of church history.

The topography of the church history that I studied was almost exclusively orography—it was concerned mostly with the mountains and mountain chains. Since historians looked to the past as if looking from atop a mountain, what they saw was other mountain peaks—peaks often arranged along a chain stretching from the horizon to the historian's own peak. As we looked at the fourth century, we saw Athanasius struggling against all odds in defense of the Nicene faith. But we paid little attention to the host of people, mostly Copts or native Egyptians, who supported him and who made his cause defensible. We knew that when things got too difficult he hid among the monks of the desert. But we paid little attention to the background from which those monks came, or why they would wish to defy imperial decrees in order to support a bishop who was one of their own—for which reason his Greco-Roman enemies called him the "black dwarf."

As we looked at the thirteenth century, we saw Saint Francis and the emergence of his order, Saint Thomas and his imposing synthesis, the great Gothic cathedrals. But we paid very little attention to those who actually built the cathedrals, or to the peasants of Roccasecca who made it possible for the family of Saint Thomas to live as they did. We paid attention to the Fourth Lateran Council and to the manner in which it sought to guide the life of the faithful; we took note of what it said regarding the doctrine of transubstantiation; but we did not look very deeply into the actual faith and devotion of the masses of the faithful.

Likewise, we studied the Reformation under the headings of Luther, Melanchthon, Zwingli, Calvin, and a few others, and we thought we had studied the Reformation.

What we had in fact done in studying such orographic church history was to skip from mountaintop to mountaintop without ever descending into the valleys, much as a flat rock skips and bounces over the water without ever really getting wet.

We now see the shortcomings of such history in ways that were generally invisible to church historians a few generations ago. The main reason for this new vision is not that new sources have been discovered or that new methods have been developed–which they have–but rather that those who are now writing church history, and those for whom church history is being written, very often find themselves more at home in the valleys than on the mountaintops. Although Eusebius himself had experienced the years of persecution, by the time he wrote the final edition of his *Church History* he was on the mountaintop, looking at other peaks, and seeing how they all led to the summit of the Constantinian settlement.[3] Isidore was Archbishop of Seville, a member of an aristocratic family, and a friend of King Recared. Bede was placed in a monastery at the age of seven, as was often the case with the sons of the nobility, and most of his writings deal with the lives and contributions of abbots, bishops, and other leaders. At the time of the Reformation and the Catholic-Protestant polemics, Baronius, the great Catholic historian, was a cardinal, and probably would have become pope had it not been for the opposition of the crown of Spain. On the Protestant side, the Centuriators of Magdeburg, although not as aristocratic as Baronius, were nevertheless interested mostly in the peaks of church history, and especially in showing that Luther was the highest peak of all.[4]

There is a sense in which this is inevitable. For a number of reasons the extant sources tend to reflect more the life and thought of the towering figures than the devotion and everyday lives of the masses. In order to study history, one has to master a number of tools that can only be mastered from a position of privilege—merely to have the time and opportunity to study Latin and Greek, and then to study ancient texts, already defines the church historian as a person of privilege in a world in which so many are still illiterate even in their own native languages. Thus, church history by its very nature has an aristocratic inclination that cannot be avoided.

But if that inclination cannot be avoided, it can at least be recognized so that historians may seek to make allowances and corrections for that inclination, just as a geographer makes allowances for the inclination of the magnetic north. It is at this point that the presence in the field of church history of people representing voices heretofore unrepresented provides a valuable corrective. Perhaps we no longer live in the valley. Certainly, we are not poor, nor voiceless, nor absolutely cut off from all recourse to power. Yet as people of the valley with deep personal contact in the valley and an experiential understanding of its depths, we can at least remind ourselves, as well as others, that even the highest mountains rise out of valleys and that one cannot really understand a mountain system in abstraction from the valleys on which it stands.

This corrective can readily be seen in some of the emphases and directions that have developed in the field of church history in the last few decades.

A few examples may illustrate this:

First, although it is true that most of the people of color, and most women, who are engaged in the task of church history are not themselves poor, nor really powerless, it is also true that for all sorts of reasons we have a closer acquaintance with poverty and powerlessness in our own communities. The result is that many of us have begun to ask of the texts and archaeological remains of the past questions that most of our own professors would not have asked.

When I was a student at Yale, under some of the best church historians of the time, I was taught to read Ignatius of Antioch, Ambrose, John Chrysostom, and the rest of those whom we then called the "Fathers" of the Church, asking them "theological" questions. By "theological" questions I mean items such as the presence of Christ in communion, or the doctrine of the Trinity.

The question of why some are inordinately rich while others starve to death was not a theological question and therefore one that most of us never thought to ask of the "Fathers." And because we never asked, they never told us!

Today, however, church historians are asking such questions. And they are asking them not simply as "ethical" questions, apart from "theology," but as central theological questions. The result is that we are beginning to hear some of the most respected ancient Christian writers say things about wealth and its proper use and distribution that we would never have imagined. But even more, we are beginning to see that for them these matters are profoundly and urgently theological matters, deeply connected with their understandings of items such as the meaning of communion and the doctrine of the Trinity.[5]

Second, although there were some women historians in earlier generations, their numbers were not such, nor their consciousness so raised, as to force all historians to look again at the historical record to see what it said about women. In general, except for passing references to some of the early martyrs, such as Perpetua and Felicitas, or to founders of religious orders, such as Saint Clare or Saint Teresa, women remained absent from the pages of church history.

In a way, that was a true reading of much of the history of the church, for throughout the centuries all sorts of limitations have been imposed on women, who, therefore, have not been allowed to attain the visible positions of leadership usually reserved for men. But in another way it ignored the fact that presumably all through the history of the church at least half of its members have been women. It also tended to ignore those outstanding women who did attain to positions of theological and ecclesiastical leadership in spite of all forces arrayed against them. (My wife supervised a dissertation on the history of pastoral counseling in the United States whose author, a woman, was intrigued by the statement that until very recently there were very few women practitioners of pastoral counseling. The thesis gives the lie to such a statement, listing numerous women in the field as far back as the 1920s.)[6]

On this score too the topography of church history has changed radically. Much of what today's students take for granted is already a significant shift from what I studied. Examples abound. Just to mention one, my mentors at Yale taught me to admire and respect what they then called the "Three Great Cappadocians": Gregory of Nazianzen, his friend Basil of Caesarea, and Basil's brother Gregory of Nyssa. They never mentioned the other great Cappadocian who stood behind both Basil and Gregory of Nyssa, namely their sister Macrina. Today, many in the new generation of students have never heard of the "Three," but rather of the "Four" Great Cappadocians.

Third, the fact that the interlocutors have changed so as to include more people of color as well as more women has meant that church history is becoming much more interested in the daily life of Christians.[7]

It is interesting to note how long we have lived with the notion that it is possible to establish a clear separation between nature and history, and that it is history that is properly human and humankind's greatest achievement. We have even given theological justification to that view by claiming that Yahweh is a god of history, while the idols of the Canaanites were gods of nature.[8] What this view often forgets is that history cannot exist without nature. The great pyramids of Egypt could never have been built without the thousands of peasants who grew the grain to feed the laborers who built the pyramids. Thomas Aquinas could never have written his great Summa if someone had not been cooking his food. This civilization could never stand without the thousands upon thousands who take care of nature and of everyday life—the immigrants who plant the vegetables and pick the lettuce, the poor who sweat in chicken factories, the unnamed women who cook for their famous husbands, the janitors who clean the offices and the laboratories in our universities.

This blindness to the importance of "nature" as compared to "history" continues to this day. I recall a seminary professor, a very committed Christian, commenting on the absurdity that garbage collectors in his city were on strike when their salary was already almost as high as his. My response was that the garbage strike, which at that point had only lasted three days, was front-page news and was already beginning to cause serious concern to city administrators, and that if all seminary professors in that city decided to strike, hardly anyone would notice. Furthermore, teaching theology is a much more pleasant occupation than collecting garbage, and I for one, if given the choice, would rather teach theology than collect garbage. The professors, writers, and others who "make history" expect to be more appreciated and better remunerated than the trash collectors, janitors, and lettuce pickers without whom we would not long survive. Perhaps that is not the way it should be. Hopefully, we shall someday find more just ways to organize our society. But in any case, it is these often ignored people who provide the material base on which the more famous can make their way into history books.

This has always been the case. But in more recent times, precisely because of the greater participation of women, minorities, and Third World people in the task of writing history, we have become aware that to understand the history of the church it does not suffice to look at the mountains and their historic achievements. We must look also at the everyday lives of Christians.

The shifts here have been enormous. Whereas in years past our most valued sources for the study of church history were the writings of ecclesiastical leaders and the archeological remains of churches and cathedrals, we are now making more use of documents and other sources that speak to us of everyday life. The discovery of an ever increasing number of papyri in Egypt dating from ancient times,[9] the study of tax documents and population records from the Middle Ages, and an archeology much more interested in everyday life have all contributed to a changing topography in church history, one in which we are increasingly able to speak not only of bishops and cathedrals but also of small village churches and of the daily life of common, everyday lay Christians.[10]

Fourth, again because of the participation in the task of church history of people from the so-called younger churches, as well as of people of color and women, contemporary church history is having to look again at many of the practices of popular religion that a generation ago were easily dismissed as "syncretistic." Significantly, the integration of Greek philosophy into Christianity has always been considered a legitimate concern for church history, and the same is true of the assimilation of Germanic tribal customs and traditions–the latter mostly because it was thought that the Germanic tribes did little to change Christianity. After all, if the historians themselves were Christians and heir to those Germanic tribes, whatever resulted from the encounter between Germanic and Greco-Roman traditions must have been part of normative Christianity. But things were different when it came to the integration of Aztec or of African religions and customs into Christianity. These were "superstitions" not worthy of consideration–but worthy of investigation and punishment by the Inquisition.

Typically, discussions of the manner in which the native populations of the Third World appropriated Christianity focused on the danger of "syncretism." In the few instances in which church history interested itself in the encounter between, for instance, Japanese culture and Christianity, one of the main issues to be explored and debated was the degree to which Japanese Christianity assimilated elements from Shintoism or from Confucianism, and how Japanese Christians dealt with the resulting danger of syncretism.[11] Significantly, although scholars knew that similar processes had taken place in the Christianization of Europe, and that Christmas trees, Santa Claus, and Easter bunnies were their result, there was little interest in determining the degree to which such accretions had affected the very nature of Christianity in Europe.

The result of all of this was that the manner in which common people actually lived and believed their Christianity was seldom a subject for church historians. Indeed, it is difficult for us church historians, trained as we are in a discipline that, as I have already said, necessarily has an aristocratic bias, to look at the faith of the people with the full appreciation it deserves. Thus, for instance, I confess that as I read Augustine (354–430) and compare him with Gregory the Great (c.540–604), my initial reaction is to see the process from one to the other as one of decline. Augustine is sophisticated. Augustine is in dialogue with the leading philosophers of his time and of classical Greece. By comparison, Gregory is uncouth. He may be a very able administrator and an empire-builder, but he is superstitious. He believes all sorts of stories about miracles, angels, and souls of the dead being released from purgatory. Even his reading of Augustine is simplistic and unsophisticated.

In this comparative evaluation of Augustine and Gregory, I am not alone. The great historian of the early twentieth century, Adolph von Harnack, issued a similar verdict:

> The doctrine of grace taught by Pope Gregory the Great (590 to 604) shows how little Augustinianism was understood in Rome, and how confused theological

thought had become in the course of the sixth century. A more motley farrago of Augustinian formulas and crude work-religion could hardly be conceived. Gregory has nowhere uttered an original thought; he has rather at all points preserved, while emasculating, the traditional systems of doctrine, reduced to the spiritual level of a coarsely material intelligence.[12]

In more recent times, however, I have been having second thoughts on the matter. It now seems clear to me that the difference between Augustine and Gregory can only be partly explained by the changes that took place with the invasions of the so-called barbarians. Perhaps the difference has more to do with the degree to which each of them really represents the living faith of the Christian masses of his time. Indeed, as I read other materials from the fourth and fifth centuries, it is clear that the "superstitious" sort of Christianity that Gregory reflects was already quite prevalent at the time of Augustine—Augustine simply was out of touch with it, or did not appreciate it.

Perhaps ideally church history should refrain from making judgments of value. I am not sure that such should truly be our ideal. But in fact historians have traditionally made such judgments in determining that Augustine's writings are more worthy of study and discussion than Gregory's, and in determining this mostly on the basis of Augustine's greater sophistication.

With increased participation of various minorities in the field of church history, as well as in other fields, such as theology, sociology of religion, and the phenomenology of religion, we are now beginning to pay more serious attention to the faith and the religious practices of the masses, not simply as aberrations due to ignorance and superstition, but rather as a religious expression as valid as any other. Significantly, while a few years ago these matters were generally known as "popular religiosity," today they are most often called "popular religion." The implication is that the religious practices of the people are not just peripheral aberrations of a supposedly pure religion, but rather the very manner in which that religion is actually lived and believed.

In this context, Orlando Espín argues for the validity of popular Catholicism, not as an aberration, but as a religion:

Let us take Catholicism as an example. It is evident that its "virtuosi" are the theologians and the clergy (especially bishops and popes). It is the role of these specialists to define and set the limits as to what is or is not acceptable and normative in the Church. For most people, however, theological work and episcopal/papal ministry are not the common ways of participating in the religion. Most Catholics play the role of recipients of the doctrinal and liturgical production of the specialists. Nevertheless, the long history of Catholicism (in many culturally shaped ways) has witnessed the birth of parallel paths that attempt to bring the religion close to the people's needs and circumstances. Often enough these paths have re-read "official" Catholicism…and thereby produced the people's own version of the religion. This is "popular" Catholicism. It claims to be authentically Catholic, and yet it has re-interpreted the normative as set forth by the Church's "virtuosi."[13]

This is not to say that there is not an important place within the community of faith for those whose gift it is to reflect on the meaning of the faith and to relate it to the wider contexts of the society and the culture in which the church lives–those whom Espín calls the "virtuosi." Otherwise, there would be no place for a book such as this, nor for an occupation such as mine. There is indeed an important and influential place for such persons, and we do well in studying them. But it is also important to remember that they do not stand alone. Nor are they nourished only by their dialogue with other intellectuals. They are part of the community of faith that has shaped them and in which most of them still stand. Therefore, to understand a figure such as Ambrose, it does not suffice to study his philosophical sources in the writings of the Neoplatonists and the structure of the rhetoric that he learned from his teachers. To understand Ambrose, it is also important to understand the faith of a community that was willing to remain practically incarcerated for days on end singing hymns in order to prevent a church from falling into the hands of a rival faction; to appreciate his conviction that when his brother Satyrus was shipwrecked, what saved him from drowning was a piece of consecrated bread that he carried on a chain hanging from his neck; and to realize that he was convinced that an ominous power dwelt in the holy relics of Saints Gervasius and Protasius.

The point is not whether Ambrose was right or wrong in believing that the sacred host had saved his brother. The point is that most historians of the nineteenth and early twentieth centuries were certainly wrong in believing that we could understand the theology of Ambrose, and his importance for the life of the church, while discounting this and other "superstitions."

I still remember studying the Trinitarian controversies of the fourth century almost forty years ago, and the reaction of the class when the professor quoted Gregory of Nazianzen's comment that one could not get one's shoes fixed without getting into a discussion as to whether the Son was homoousios or homoiousios with the Father. The professor quoted Gregory with a chuckle, and we also chuckled in disdain at an age so fanatical that people would fight over a mere iota.

Today I chuckle at the naïveté, not of Gregory's age, but of my own, that we were so simple as to believe that we could understand Gregory's time without at least trying to understand why that particular iota appeared so important to them. The Trinitarian controversies, I am increasingly convinced, were not over difficult and arcane matters of philosophical theology, nor even over formulae that our supposedly unsophisticated ancestors took too literally, but over ways of living the faith that affected people in their everyday lives. If in Gregory's time the common people in a cobbler's shop were eager to get into the argument over the iota in homoiousios, this is a sign that we probably have not understood what was actually at stake from their point of view. Until we can understand the everyday connections of the doctrine of the Trinity as people saw them in the fourth century, we will be far from understanding those controversies about which so much has been written!

The changing topography of church history thus forces us to look anew not only at issues such as the role of women in the life of the church, Christian understandings of wealth and poverty, and everyday Christian devotion and practice, but also at some of the items that have always been central to the history of Christianity.

Cartographic Changes

Finally, the changing topography of church history also implies some changes in cartography. Perhaps the clearest example of this is in the manner in which the present topography of the church in the United States challenges the traditional cartography of American church history. That cartography—the one that was followed when I first studied the history of the church in this country—began in New England, and progressively moved south and west.

A case in point is Sydney Ahlstrom's now classic book *A Religious History of the American People*—a book that was being written at Yale precisely as I was there, taking some of my early steps in the study of church history. A quick glance at the Table of Contents of that two-volume work suffices to show the cartography that stands behind it.

The first of nine parts into which that book is divided is devoted to the "European Prologue"—as if the original inhabitants of these lands had no religion. As part of that prologue, Ahlstrom includes a section on "The Church in New Spain." Near the end of that section he concludes:

> The marks of Spanish Catholicism on American religious and cultural life were…deeply etched. Aside from the large Spanish-speaking ethnic minority in the United States, much of which has come from Puerto Rico and Cuba as well as from Mexico, considerable weight must be given to the place that old imperial Spain occupies in the consciousness of all Americans, though especially of Roman Catholics. Because the federal Union came to include most of the Spanish borderlands, many Americans can draw sustenance from the fact that the country's oldest heritage is not Puritan but Catholic.[14]

Significantly, however, after that statement part 2 turns to the Puritans of New England, and from that point on the story goes on as if practically nothing had been happening in the West and Southwest. Much later, in a section on the growth of Roman Catholicism devoted mostly to Irish immigration, there is one page on the consequences of the Mexican-American War for that denomination. But even that section deals mostly with how the hierarchy was organized, and says nothing of the actual religion of the Mexican population that had been incorporated into the North American Roman Catholic Church.

When this book was published, it was correctly acclaimed as a masterpiece in bringing together the many strands of American religious history. Yet today, not even a third of a century later, it is clear that its map of American church history is no longer adequate. The new topography, which includes a Hispanic constituency that is approximately half of all Roman Catholics in the country, as well as a sizable and growing number of Protestants, has radically changed the cartography. There are now increasing demands that North American religious history include the *penitentes* of New Mexico, the saga of Antonio José Martínez and his clashes with Archbishop Lamy, and the struggles of Hispanic Protestants to find their own way of being Protestant. Furthermore, since there are indications that some of the early colonizers of what was then northern Mexico were crypto-Jews, or at least Catholics of Jewish heritage, and that it was among some of these that Protestantism first made headway, this change in cartography is significant, not only for the history of the Christian church in the United States but even for the history of Judaism. To this must now be added the growing presence in the United States of Islam, Buddhism, Hinduism, and other religions, so that "a religious history of the American people" becomes an entirely different enterprise than when Ahlstrom wrote his masterpiece.

As this case shows, changes in topography are closely linked to and even result in changes in cartography. When the story is told by Hispanic Americans, the West gains a prominence that it did not have when the story was told almost exclusively by Anglo-Saxon males. Likewise, when the same story is told by African Americans, it is the South that gains new prominence.

But that is not all. When cartography and topography change, what is taking place is a series of transformations of enormous proportions. Continents shift. Ocean depths rise to the surface. New mountain ranges lift up their heads. It is to such cataclysmic changes that the next chapter turns.

3

Cataclysmic Changes

Having discussed the changing cartography and topography of church history, it is time to add a third element to the changing geography of church history–the element of time. Although we tend to think of geography in spatial terms, and of history in temporal terms, the truth is that the Earth also has a history. The Earth also changes over time. Some of these changes we call cataclysmic. These are changes of enormous proportions, as when land masses disappear or others emerge from the bottom of the ocean. These are the changes perhaps dimly remembered in the ancient legends of Atlantis. They are the changes studied by geologists, seismologists, and others. Out of them have emerged new mountains and new valleys, new land masses and new oceans.

Geologists tell us that there was a time when the Great Plains were under water, and perhaps also a time when the Mediterranean was dry. Likewise, the changes that are taking place in church history during our generation are lifting up entire centuries and events previously submerged in lack of interest, and making other centuries and events much less important than they used to appear.

The Great Continents of Church History

When I first studied church history, there were four climactic moments in the history of the church: the conversion of Constantine in the fourth century, with its attendant age of the great "Fathers" of the church; the high point of the Middle Ages in the thirteenth century; the Reformation of the sixteenth; and the theological developments of the nineteenth. In the field of historical theology, if you knew quite well the theologians of those four centuries—the fourth, the thirteenth, the sixteenth, and the nineteenth—you knew all that was really necessary to know. These were, so to speak, the four great continents, the four great land masses of church history. What happened in between those four great continents was of lesser importance.

Between the time of Jesus and that of Constantine, we studied history in order to see the island chain, and eventually the isthmus, that connected the early church with Constantine. It was not difficult to read the first three centuries of the history of the church in that manner, for that was how Eusebius described them—and Eusebius was the teacher of us all.

Between the time of Constantine and his immediate successors, and the great flourishing of the thirteenth century, there was a tempestuous sea of invasions and obscurantism. First came the Germanic invasions. Then followed the Arabs, and the Norse, and the Slavs, and the Magyars. Each of these wreaked havoc on an important portion of Christendom, until Christian civilization began to emerge again out of the turbulent seas early in the twelfth century, in order to reach its pinnacle in the thirteenth.

However, just as the land masses of the Americas rise slowly out of the ocean in the eastern coasts, reach their high point far to the west, and then suddenly plunge into the other ocean, so did this flourishing of the thirteenth century plunge into a new ocean of corruption, ignorance, and superstition until once again it reached the verdant land of the Reformation in the sixteenth century.

After that came the twin seas of rationalism and Protestant orthodoxy, both very different, and yet very similar. In the middle of them arose various forms of Pietism, Methodism, Moravianism—some would say as islands of renewal, some would say as new disturbances in already unsettled waters.

Eventually, however, out of both rationalism and orthodoxy, and reacting to both, emerged the great theologians of the nineteenth century. There were high peaks in the land: Schleiermacher, Troeltsch, Ritschl, Harnack. Of these and other giants, most of them German, we were the lesser heirs whose task it was to study and emulate them.

That was the configuration of the great land masses of church history as I first studied it. Again, four centuries were of paramount importance, like so many continents in the oceans: the fourth, the thirteenth, the sixteenth, and the nineteenth.

Continental Shifts: The Emergence of the Second Century

Now a series of events and considerations are forcing me and other historians to look elsewhere for the great land masses—and this to such a point that I can find no better way to describe the change in our perspective than as cataclysmic.

First of all, the period prior to Constantine, the second and third centuries, is rapidly emerging as an entire new continent that merits more and new exploration. This certainly was not an unknown period in church history. On the contrary, since it was deemed to be formative, and since there were relatively few written sources for its study, it has always been fairly well known. The extant documents of the time have been read and reread and examined in painstaking detail, to the point that one would think that there was nothing new to be discovered in them. Ph.D. students seeking subjects for dissertations on patristics had to look for ever more obscure details in order to fulfill the traditional requirement that a dissertation must be original and contribute something new to the existing body of knowledge. For a while, one way to find something new in these documents was to discuss their connection with various religious and philosophical currents of the times. Was Ignatius influenced by mystery religions? Were his opponents gnostics? Or did they represent some obscure Jewish sect? Were they Jewish gnostics? Was Ignatius himself influenced by gnosticism? What is the rhetorical structure of First Clement, and how does it relate to classical rhetorical theory?

Another way to find something original to say was to apply to the texts of the second century the sort of historico-critical analysis that had become common in biblical studies. Are there actually two documents in Polycarp's letter to the Philippians? What is the date of the Didache? Did the document of the Two Ways, which appears both in the Didache and in Pseudo-Barnabas, ever circulate as an independent document? How was the Shepherd of Hermas compiled? How many layers of tradition can be found in it?

While many of these questions are important, and the answers given to them must be taken into account in any rereading of the second century, they generally take for granted that we have a fairly good picture of the second century and its significance, that no new major reinterpretation is necessary, and that the received wisdom as to the general tenor of Christianity during that period suffices and need not be questioned.

But in fact, today many are beginning to question the traditional interpretation of the second and third centuries. In brief, and with some oversimplification, one could say that the traditional interpretation of the second and third centuries was bequeathed to us by Eusebius and the entire school of church history that followed in his footsteps. When Eusebius looked at the second and third centuries, he looked at them from the standpoint of the Constantinian settlement, and thus saw them as preparation for that settlement, which was the culmination of Christian history.[1]

Today, however, as the map of Christianity and therefore of church history changes, many are wondering whether the fourth century and the Constantinian settlement are as valuable a paradigm as we were initially told. That question is being asked most forcefully by persons outside the traditional centers—centers that, like Eusebius, benefitted from the Constantinian settlement and its later modifications. In Latin America, for instance, where a commitment on the part of many Christians to the cause of the poor has led to many a death, there is a growing awareness that perhaps the early martyrs died not because the government did not understand the nature of their faith, but rather, because the government understood it all too well. In this country, a former student of mine has recently written a dissertation on the subversive elements in the visions of the early martyrs—subversive of the structures both of the Empire and of the church.[2] Significantly, the person writing this dissertation is a woman and a Hispanic. From the margins, Latin American historians, as well as this woman and many others, are rediscovering the significance of the second and third centuries, not as building toward the fourth, but rather as a time when Christians were marginal to a society that opposed their views and therefore persecuted them. For such Christians, who may well be the majority of Christians in the world, the second and third centuries are in many ways paradigmatic of their own situation and emerge with cataclysmic force, almost as a new continent arising from the bottom of the ocean.

Furthermore, when seen from this perspective, the second and third centuries become important not only for those who are sufficiently marginal to be open to see the subversiveness of Christianity but also for a growing segment of the church that finds itself increasingly marginalized as the last remnants of the Constantinian settlement disappear. Even in the traditional centers of Christianity in the North Atlantic, churches can no longer take for granted the support of society at large. Most of them lost the support of the state long ago. That certainly was the case in the United States. But now they are also losing the support of society at large. Here in the United States, even long after the separation of church and state had been made a matter of constitutional law and political dogma, there was a general sense that the values of the society roughly corresponded to, or at least supported, the values of the church. Churches were generally content with leaving most of the education of children, as well as much of what traditionally had been their charitable work, to the educational and welfare programs of the state. Just a few decades ago, when the so-called mainline churches spoke on civil issues, people listened. When Reinhold Niebuhr spoke on pressing political issues, the political powers at least acted as if they were listening. Perhaps, as Niebuhr's brother Richard suggested, Christ the transformer of culture was at work in this country.

Now that time and its illusions have passed, the values that the society at large, and especially its mass media, promote are far from Christian values. Christians are increasingly aware that they no longer live in a Christian society–if they ever did.

The reaction of the Christian right is well known. In essence, the Christian right reflects a nostalgia for the Constantinian past– or at least for an idealized and simplified Constantinian past. In some areas–notably the United States–the Christian right is sufficiently well organized and well funded that it has already made significant inroads in the political process, and may even attain to greater success. Its agenda is clear: to legislate so that society is organized according to what it deems to be Christian standards, leading to the establishment of a Christian culture. Since this—or the appearance thereof—was one of the most notable results of the Constantinian settlement, it is apparent that the goal of the Christian right is somehow to return to the general features of that settlement.

What is not equally apparent, because it does not make news as a bomb in an abortion clinic does, is that many other Christians are coming to positions that are very similar to those of their spiritual ancestors of the second and third centuries. That was a time when the church was still at the margin of society, and its lessons have become particularly relevant for a new time in which the church once again finds itself at the margin. For such Christians, what the changing political and cultural situation offers is not so much a call to return to a past time of Christian hegemony as the opportunity to learn more of what it means to be a people of faith in circumstances in which such faith is not supported by the surrounding society and culture—in other words, a time like the second and third centuries. As a result, many Christian churches are recovering elements of Christian life and worship that were characteristic of those earlier times.

This may be seen most clearly in the manner in which more and more churches are reclaiming elements in the liturgies of the second and third centuries that had long been forgotten. To take a single example, one may look at the renunciations that were so prominent a feature in early baptismal rites, and notice how they have made their way back into the more recent baptismal rites of a number of major denominations in the United States.

The following words from the order for baptism in the Presbyterian *Book of Common Worship* are a case in point. They are to be pronounced immediately before the Creed:

> Do you renounce all evil,
> and powers in the world
> which defy God's righteousness and love?
> **I renounce them**.
> Do you renounce the ways of sin

That separate you from the love of God?
I renounce them.[3]

And in my own United Methodist ritual:

> On behalf of all the church, I ask you:
> Do you renounce the spiritual forces of wickedness,
> reject the evil powers of this world,
> and repent of your sin?
> **I do.**
> Do you accept the freedom and power God gives you
> to resist evil, injustice, and oppression
> in whatever form they present themselves?
> **I do.**[4]

These words, which did not appear in the earlier rituals of either denomination and which are reminiscent of early Christian baptismal rites, have been added in part as a result of relatively recent studies in the history of worship, but also because at least some North American churches in the latter half of the twentieth century were becoming aware that if one is steeped in the mainstream culture of this society, there is much which one must renounce as one accepts baptism into the body of Christ. And that was also the case of people in the Roman Empire in the second and third centuries who decided to join the Christian church.

Similarly, a few decades ago churches were content with one hour in Sunday school as their main and almost sole opportunity to teach the faith to upcoming generations. After all, it was thought, a great deal of what is being taught at school and by society at large is also part of Christian education. Today that is no longer the case. Churches are exploring dimensions of worship as contributing not only to education but also to Christian identity and to the formation of Christian character. Some churches are developing more intentional educational programs, both for children and for adults, in which they seek to undo or to counteract much of the ethos of the surrounding society—an ethos that they see as characterized by consumerism, egotism, hedonism, and materialism.

What is true of the churches in North America, where there is still a remnant of social and cultural support for Christianity, is much more so for the churches in the newly expanded map of Christianity, many of which exist in lands where they not only lack support but also often meet open opposition from the dominant culture.

Thus, once again, the second and third centuries are emerging from the shadow of the fourth as particularly important for the church in the twenty-first. This amounts to no less than a cataclysmic change in the geography of church history, as if an entire continent were emerging from the bottom of the sea.

Continental Shifts: The Emergence of the Seventh and Eighth Centuries

Another period that has emerged with cataclysmic force is the latter part of the seventh century and the eighth century. Mohammed died in Medina in 632, and a hundred years later, at the battle of Tours (or Poitiers), the advance of Islam into Western Europe was halted. In those hundred years, the new faith and its armies had conquered both the ancient Persian Empire—to the very borders of India—and most of the traditional centers of Christianity, such as Jerusalem, Antioch, Alexandria, and Carthage. Its armies had crossed the Strait of Gibraltar in 711 and put an end to the Visigothic kingdom of Spain. The Byzantinian Empire, deprived of most of its territories, would endure for another seven centuries, but it would never regain its former glory and power. The Mediterranean, until then a Christian lake, was now divided between Christianity and Islam—the latter having absolute control of large portions of it. Meanwhile, in Northern Europe, Christianity was becoming increasingly Germanized and was distancing itself from its ancient Mediterranean and Near Eastern roots. Forced by political circumstances to seek the support of the Franks, the popes turned increasingly to the North, and away from the Byzantine East.[5]

All this we always knew. We simply did not generally realize its importance. Already in the first half of the twentieth century Henri Pirenne had argued that the true dividing line between antiquity and the Middle Ages was not the fall of Rome to the Goths in 410, but rather, the period of Mohammed and Charlemagne.[6] But historians in general, and church historians in particular, continued to regard 410 as the great moment of transition. It was at that point that classical Roman antiquity received its death blow, and it became clear that the "barbarians" from the North were the new power. Since at the time of the Renaissance it was mostly the descendants of those "barbarians" who wrote and interpreted history, and who now thought that the great task at hand was the recovery of classical antiquity, it became customary to set the year 410 as the great watershed and to dub everything from then until the Renaissance as the "Middle Ages"– that is, the period between the glories of classical antiquity and the glories of the Renaissance. The advance of Islam was then one more of the many tragic occurrences of those "dark ages." It is thus that Williston Walker introduces a brief paragraph in which he outlines the Arab conquests:

> Justinian's brilliant restoration of the Roman power was but of brief duration. From 568, the Lombards were pressing into Italy. Without conquering it wholly, they occupied the north and a large portion of the center. The last Roman garrisons were driven out of Spain by the Visigoths in 624. The Persians gained temporary control of Syria, Palestine, and Egypt between 613 and 629, and overran Asia Minor and the Bosphorus. On the European side, the Avars, and the Slavic Croats and Serbs, conquered the Danube lands and most of the Balkan provinces, largely annihilating Christianity there, penetrating in 623 and 626 to the defenses of Constantinople itself. That the empire did not perish was due to the military genius of Emperor Heraclius (610–642), by whom the Persians were brilliantly defeated, and the lost provinces restored. Before his death, however, a new power, that of Mohammed-anism, had arisen.[7]

This gives the impression that the advance of Islam, although a serious challenge to Christianity, was not very different from the threats posed by Lombards, Avars, or Croats. It was part of the chaos and decadence that had begun more than two hundred years earlier.

Today we look at things differently. If we do not understand those events of the seventh and eighth centuries–as well as the continued conflicts of the Crusades, colonialism, and so forth–we shall never understand the events of the twenty-first symbolized in the attacks on the Twin Towers in New York. Today there are few conflicts that stem from the fall of Rome in 410, but there are many that stem from that vast confrontation of the seventh and eighth centuries and the continued confrontation after that.

Thus, once again, a period that seemed to be submerged in the vast ocean of the Middle Ages emerges as a vast and relatively unexplored continent that historians have to take into account.

Continental Shifts: A New Tilt to the Sixteenth Century

In other cases, periods that we used to consider important for particular reasons have now become important for entirely different reasons. A case in point is the sixteenth century. Fifty years ago, the sixteenth century was important because it was the period of the Protestant Reformation; but today, because of the changing cartography of church history, I can no longer ignore the fact that the sixteenth century is not only the time of the Protestant Reformation but also of the Spanish conquest of the Western Hemisphere. This is part of the changing cartography of church history. But this cartographic change is nothing short of cataclysmic, for it is closely related to a number of developments in recent decades that have radically changed our view of the sixteenth century.

When I first studied church history, the Protestant Reformation appeared as the great watershed in the history of Western Christianity, in part because the gulf between Protestantism and Roman Catholicism was still almost at its widest point. That point had come in the late nineteenth century and had relatively little to do with the issues of the sixteenth. Indeed, the main reason for the growing distance between Protestantism and Roman Catholicism had to do mostly with their contrasting reactions to the modern world.

Roman Catholicism reacted with official and unequivocal rejection of most that was modern. The *Syllabus of Errors* proclaimed by Pius IX in 1864 expressed quite well the mood of a hierarchy reacting against the losses that the church had suffered with the advent of modernity. The last of the eighty errors listed summarizes quite well the mood of the entire document, as well as of the leadership of the Catholic church at the time. The last error, unequivocally condemned by the pope, is that "the Roman pontiff can and ought to reconcile and agree with progress, with liberalism, and with modern civilization."[8] Ten years before that, in an attempt to show his muscle in the definition of doctrine, Pope Pius had promulgated the dogma of the immaculate conception of Mary. Six years after the *Syllabus of Errors*, in 1870, he and all popes were declared infallible by the First Vatican Council. Significantly, two months and two days after this proclamation, Pope Pius lost Rome to the Republic of Italy. Thus, at a time when the papacy was losing political power, it tended to balance things out by insisting on its spiritual and doctrinal authority. Such was the mood of Roman Catholicism in the nineteenth century and during the first half of the twentieth. Along those lines, let us not forget that it was Pius XII, in 1950, who proclaimed the dogma of the bodily assumption of Mary, and that as recently as the electoral campaign of John F. Kennedy many liberal Protestants wondered whether a Roman Catholic could ever be president of this country.

Meanwhile, Protestantism was moving in exactly the opposite direction. If Roman Catholicism was perhaps guilty of an excessive animosity toward modernity, Protestantism, especially in its leading theologians, came to see itself as the religion of modernity. In spite of their many differences, the one point that Schleiermacher, Hegel, Troeltsch, Ritschl, and Harnack had in common was that all of them, each in his own way and within his own system, believed that the superiority of Protestantism over Catholicism was proven by its compatibility with modernity.

Thus, it is not surprising that when I first studied the history of the church, it was taken for granted that the sixteenth century was the great watershed in that history and that its significance lay in the Reformation and the permanent division of the church that it caused. Although by the time I began graduate school there were signs that things were changing, it was not until I had begun teaching that those changes became apparent, especially in the papacy of John XXIII and the Second Vatican Council.

However, it is not only in the Roman Catholic communion that things have changed. As modernity began to give signs of its own weaknesses, Protestantism also began to reassess its own self-understanding. This process, which began as early as Karl Barth and has not yet run its course, will lead to unpredictable consequences. But one thing is certain: Protestantism no longer sees itself as yoked to the fortunes of modernity. Thus, as the twentieth century drew to a close, and probably modernity with it, the gulf between Protestant and Catholic seemed to be narrowing.

This is not to say that all differences and even clashes have been overcome. Right now, in Latin America, there is a great contest between Roman Catholicism and a new sort of Protestantism that has made enormous strides, to the point that what is at stake is probably nothing less than the religious allegiance of the continent. Needless to say, in the heat of such a battle the differences between Catholic and Protestant are exacerbated, and the conflict becomes as virulent as any debate in the nineteenth century.

Still, as I look at the picture of the worldwide church and try to divine what the third millennium might bring, I become increasingly convinced that in our evaluation of the sixteenth century the Reformation will eventually take second place to the Spanish and Portuguese invasion of the Western Hemisphere, and to the ensuing colonial expansion of Western Europe. That was the first of two momentous stages in the birth of a worldwide church—and in many ways the birth of such a church will be proven to be more significant for the future history of the church catholic than the birth of the Lutheran, the Reformed, the Tridentine, or any other tradition stemming from the Reformation. One could thus say that the cataclysmic change that has affected our view of the sixteenth century is such that, although that century still looms large and must still be listed as such, an entire new mountain chain has emerged that tends to overshadow the older—much as in this North American continent the younger Rockies overshadow the older Appalachians.

Continental Shifts: A New Tilt to the Nineteenth Century

Since I have mentioned Protestant theology in the nineteenth century, one must add that something similar is already happening with our reading of that century. When I first studied church history, what was important about that period was the long list of outstanding theologians who dealt with a wide variety of issues posed by modernity. Today, however, I tend to look at the nineteenth century as significant primarily because it was the second stage in the birth of the universal church. Significantly, the impact of the great theologians of the nineteenth century has generally been waning, while the impact of the churches founded in Asia, Africa, and Latin America during that century has been growing ever since. Thus, both the sixteenth century and the nineteenth are undergoing cataclysmic changes in the minds of church historians.

Geography Has a History

My friends and students are often surprised when I tell them that the subject I most disliked in my early schooling was history. Now I know that part of the reason was that I did not relate history to geography, so events and names and movements appeared in the pages of history in a vacuum, as if floating in mid-air. Given that approach, my incomprehension of and consequent dislike for church history are not surprising.

The counterpart of that is that I also did not like geography. Geography was a series of maps to study and long lists to memorize and to place on the map: mountains, lakes, rivers, islands, volcanoes, nations, cities, capitals, borders, and so on. I did not like geography because it was too rigid, too set, because it had no movement.

Today, my next favorite subject for study, after history, is geography. The reason is simple: not only have I learned that history has a geography, but also that geography has a history. Just as history must be understood in the context of the geography in which it occurs, so must geography be understood as a changing reality. I well remember the map of Africa I studied years ago. It was a map with the allure of faraway places—so far away that many of them no longer exist: Rhodesia, French Equatorial Africa, the Belgian Congo. These have all disappeared. In their stead other places have appeared: Zimbabwe, Namibia, Zaire, Burkina Fasso. In my own lifetime, I have seen geography change prodigiously. And if geography has a history, this means that a new reading of history may also be subversive of the present reading of geography; that a reading of the history of national borders, for instance, reminds us that all existing borders are the result of historical circumstances; that just as all mountains are eventually eroded, the present topography of any society is at best provisional; that just as continental plates shift, so do centers of power and influence.

That is what I find exciting about church history and its changing geography. It is what I find exciting, but also what I find terrifying, as each day the history I learned yesterday has to be relearned. That is probably what makes it so difficult for so many historians to acknowledge the new configurations of the emerging geography. Yet if any should be able to survive such cataclysmic changes, it should be those of us who claim to be heirs to the faith of the psalmist who long ago sang: "God is our refuge and strength, a very present help in trouble. Therefore we will not fear, though the earth should change, though the mountains shake in the heart of the sea" (Ps. 46:1–2).

4

The Failing Map of Modernity

An Old, but Familiar Map

The speaker was one of the most distinguished theologians in a certain denomination in this country. He was addressing a Sunday school class on the subject of evangelism and the Reformed tradition, and he proudly stated that "the ethos and form of government of our church are so rich and so carefully nuanced, that one has to be born into it, or even better, come from a long line of members of the same denomination, in order to participate in it fully."

My first reaction was one of disbelief at the implied contradiction between the subject and what was being said. The subject was evangelism. We were being invited to go out and tell others the good news. Yet that good news somehow involved also an invitation to join a Christian community in which perhaps after a couple of generations the descendants of today's converts might begin to feel at home!

Then my reaction turned to sadness. I grew up in an environment in which the evangelistic imperative was foremost in the life of the church. And now I was saddened that a denomination that had so much to offer to others was so engrossed in its own inner life as to turn its very ethos and system of governance into an obstacle for others to come to belief.

Sadness gave way to anger. I was angry at the implied racism and ethnocentrism of such a statement. What that theologian was actually implying was that in order to be a fully participating member of his denomination, which to him was also the highest form of Christianity, you had to be able to trace your family roots back to the land from whence his ancestors came.

Slowly, however, my anger subsided, as I came to realize that had I heard a similar statement when I was growing up as a Protestant in Cuba, I would not have been at all surprised. Indeed, I probably would have agreed at least with part of it. That may be difficult for most of my readers to understand. I confess that it is even difficult for me to believe. But the fact is that I, and millions of others like me throughout the world, grew up with an intellectual map in which that theologian's statement would have been received with a measure of agreement and even enthusiasm.

As I was growing up as a Protestant in Cuba, there were a number of elements that came together to give shape to my Protestantism and indeed to my entire worldview. There certainly was the conviction that Protestantism was closer to scripture than the Roman Catholic faith of my peers. But there was also a geopolitical worldview—an ideological map of the world—that generally went with being a Protestant. It was a worldview dramatically presented in a book I still remember having read in my early teens, a book entitled *Protestant Imperialism,* by an Alsatian Reformed author by the name of Frédéric Hoffet.[1] According to Hoffet, all the more advanced nations in the world were Protestant. Catholic nations lagged far behind in items such as literacy, freedom, and democracy. I remember reading that book and thinking that my efforts to convert my friends and peers were not just a religious task but also a patriotic one. By bringing Protestantism to my land, I was bringing not only the true faith but also the solution to the political and civil corruption that we all bemoaned.

Needless to say, today I look at matters quite differently. Today I know that corruption in my country was caused not only by faulty ethical teaching within but also and most importantly by significant investments and other forms of intervention by very Protestant interests and investors from outside. Today I would argue that much of what we have traditionally called "underdevelopment" is in fact misdevelopment, and that the contrast among nations today is not between "developed" and "underdeveloped," but rather between "developers" and "developees."

But that is not the point. The point is that as I look around me and suddenly come to realize the enormous changes that have taken place in my worldview, I discover that similar changes have taken place throughout the world. Again, the map of Africa that I studied in high school no longer exists. In Europe itself the map has also changed. I grew up with a map of Europe whose names emphasized unity and hid diversity: Yugoslavia, Czechoslovakia, the Union of Soviet Socialist Republics. Now those unities have come apart: Macedonia, Bosnia, Serbia, Croatia, Slovakia, Ukraine, Armenia. The Caribbean in which I grew up boasted three independent nations: Cuba, the Dominican Republic, and Haiti. Today they are too many to count.

It is not just the political maps of Africa, Europe, and the Caribbean that have changed. It is also the entire mental map with which I grew up, the mental map that was dominant at the end of the Second World War. One could say that a vast earthquake is shaking the whole world, physical and mental, so that entire portions of our traditional maps are being erased or at least brought into question.

The worst part of all of this, what makes the new situation most difficult for all of us, is that the previous world map has not been replaced by a single map on which we all agree. This is true of the political map, as wars in the former Yugoslavia and in the former Soviet Union indicate. Indeed, there are predictions that the next fifty years will see the rise of a hundred and fifty new independent nations—mostly in Africa and Asia, but also in Europe and perhaps even in North America.

The Map of Modernity

What is true of the political map is even more so of the intellectual map. The intellectual map with which most of us grew up was the program of modernity. Although there is no general agreement on many details, there are some characteristics of modernity that seem undeniable.

The first such characteristic is modernity's quest for objective knowledge. This may be seen in the two great revolutions that mark the beginning of modernity: the Copernican and the Cartesian. What Copernicus proposed was not simply a new understanding of the solar system and the movement of the planets. What Copernicus proposed was a radical shift in perspective–a shift that eventually became the hallmark of modernity. Whereas the ancient Ptolemaic system explained the movement of the heavenly bodies as seen from an observer on Earth, what Copernicus advanced was a description of the solar system as seen by a theoretical independent observer outside that system. Some readers may remember the models of the solar system that our generation studied in school: miniature replicas, with handles and pulleys, that we could watch from above, as outside observers. That was the result and the sign of the Copernican revolution. Had we lived before that revolution and tried to depict the solar system in a similar model, we would have been at the center, with spheres revolving all around us. We would have seen nothing wrong with putting ourselves, the observers, at the very center of things. It was the Copernican revolution that shifted our entire mental map, so that knowledge and objectivity started to go together, while knowledge and subjectivity were polar opposites.

Then came the Cartesian revolution. The four points of the famous *Method* of Descartes hoped to provide a system by which to make certain that nothing was taken as true that could not undeniably, indubitably be proven to be so. Thus, Cartesian doubt is grounded on the unshakable faith that objective knowledge is not only possible, but even the only sort of knowledge worthy of the name.

Objectivity leads to the next great pillar of the modern program: universality. The knowledge after which the modern mind seeks is universal in two ways: first, it is all-encompassing; second, it is capable of being recognized by any rational being whose vision is not obscured by the "idols of the tribe." Let us look at these in order.

First, the universal scope of knowledge. Descartes himself expresses this quite clearly in the fourth point of his method, which is "always to make enumerations so complete, and reviews so general, that I would be certain that nothing was omitted."[2]

In the explanation that follows, Descartes does make an exception by declaring that he is referring only to "all things which can fall under human knowledge." He was an alumnus of the famous Collège de la Fleche, and as such was not totally ignorant of theology or of what theologians said about mysteries such as the Trinity and the Incarnation. Nor was he ignorant of the possible consequences of stepping beyond the bounds of Roman Catholic orthodoxy, and he hoped that this phrase would safeguard him. Still, the heroic arrogance of the statement has prompted the following words from Spanish philosopher José Ortega y Gasset:

> What joy! What a tone of energetic challenge to the universe! What an arrogant petulance in these magnificent words of Descartes! Now you know: Apart from the divine mysteries, which he has the courtesy to set aside, for this man there is no mystery that cannot be solved…At last, we shall know the truth about all things.[3]

This universal reach of the method of objective, rational analysis leads to the second aspect of its universality: its conclusions can be recognized as perfectly logical and objective by all rational beings, no matter where or in what circumstances. Remember that Descartes began his *Discourse on Method* by stating, with some sense of humor, that common sense must be the best distributed thing on Earth, for even those who are most difficult to please in other things, and are always asking for more, seem to be content with the sense they already have. It is on this common sense, on this universal reason, that Descartes plans to build his system, with the clear implication that any who do not accept it must simply be lacking in common sense.

This was the mental map with which most of us grew up. It was the mental map of the modern age. It was the mental map that made it possible for me to read a book such as Hoffet's *Protestant Imperialism* and simply accept the judgment of an Alsatian pastor over my own culture, blaming all our political, economic, and social shortcomings on that culture, claiming that the Protestant North Atlantic was much better in all respects, and claiming further that the reason for this was its Protestant faith. In a word, I had been internally colonized by a mental world map in which there could only be one rational, objectively better, universally valid way of doing things, of seeing the world, and of organizing life. And that one rational, objectively better, universally valid way was the way of the Protestant North Atlantic.

When I say that I had been "colonized," I have chosen my words with care, for there is a connection between the modern vision of the world and the also modern colonial enterprise. Copernicus published his work *On the Revolution of the Celestial Spheres* in 1530. The first modern atlas of the world, the *Orbis Terrarum* of Ortelius, was published in 1570. Two thirds of a century later, in 1637, Descartes published his *Discourse on Method.* The apple fell on Isaac Newton's garden in 1665. All this coincided with the first great period of European colonial expansion, dominated by the Spanish and the Portuguese, in which the British and others also joined at a slightly later date.

Then came the second great wave of modernity, when the principles of Newton and others were applied to technological development. Preparation for this second phase took most of the eighteenth century. Thus, although the earliest prototype for a steam engine was built in 1690, it was not until 1819 that the first steamship crossed the Atlantic. The steamship, capable of carrying goods, ideas, troops, and missionaries with surprising swiftness, became the symbol and the means for a new era in which the North Atlantic seemed to have become the center of the world. That second wave of modernity was paralleled by a second wave of colonial expansion—now led by the British and the French, but also joined by the Germans, the Dutch, and the Italians. The map of Africa changed drastically. In 1800, most of Africa was unknown to the Europeans, who considered it a "dark continent." By 1914, with the partition of Africa, most of it belonged to European powers. Similar changes took place in southern Asia, where the British became masters of the Indian subcontinent, and where the only independent state left in Indochina was Siam, which acted as a buffer between British interests to the west and the French to the east. Eventually even China became part of the world colonial map. In the Western Hemisphere the changes were no less drastic. Impelled by the examples of the United States and the French revolutions, the Spanish colonies in the hemisphere proclaimed their independence, only to give rise to a new age of economic neocolonialism that has not yet ended. In North America, the thirteen British colonies that originally occupied only the rim of the Atlantic rapidly expanded westward, conquering and purchasing lands formerly belonging to Native Americans, to the French, to Mexico, and others. In all this, the ideological driving forces were, as the British would say, the "white man's burden" to civilize and modernize the rest of the world; or, as North Americans would say, the "manifest destiny" of their nation to do likewise at least as far as the coast of the Pacific. Thus, one could argue that, as Indian scholar Ashis Nandy has said, colonialism is the "armed version" of modernity.[4]

What we often forget is that all this is closely entwined with the history of Christianity, and in particular with Protestantism. In 1521, when Luther stood before the Emperor at the Diet of Worms, Hernán Cortés was beginning to consolidate his power over Mexico. Copernicus published *On the Revolution of the Celestial Spheres* the same year that the German Protestant princes signed the Confession of Augsburg. In 1536, when John Calvin was publishing the first edition of his *Institutes,* Pedro de Mendoza was founding Buenos Aires. In 1539, while Calvin was commenting on the fountain of our salvation in Romans, Hernando de Soto was looking for the fountain of youth in Florida. The *Discourse on Method* was published in Leyden in 1637, just a few years before the Westminster Assembly, and less than twenty years and twenty-five miles away from the Synod of Dort. Furthermore, if we are to believe Descartes himself, his great discovery came much earlier, in 1619, and therefore practically at the same time as the Synod of Dort.

The first decades of modernity—the sixteenth century—saw an unparalleled Catholic missionary expansion. That expansion was practically coextensive with Iberian conquest and colonialism. This could be called the first wave of modernity, when Western Europe first employed its technological advantage to impose its views on the rest of the world. While Roman Catholicism was claiming ever greater and more factual universality, and was using the tools of modernity to stake such claims, Protestantism was parochial in comparison, flourishing mostly in areas that remained politically divided, and Protestants clung to their traditional local and regional distinctions. At the high point of its own Catholic Reformation, the Council of Trent in 1545–63, the Roman Catholic Church sought a universal uniformity it had never had before. Therefore, in spite of all that we have been told, during the early sixteenth century Roman Catholicism was in some ways more "modern" than Protestantism.

This was true, however, only of the very first decades of modernity. Soon Protestantism became more modern than Roman Catholicism. Protestantism flourished in the nascent industrial areas of the Netherlands and Britain, which would soon lead the rest of the world into modernity. The reign of Elizabeth in England (1558–1603) marks that transition. Led first by England, and then by the United Kingdom and the Netherlands, Protestants colonized the world in an ever accelerating process that continued into the first decade of the twentieth century. Thus, if it is true that colonialism is the "armed version" of modernity, it is also true that to a very high degree Protestantism, particularly as it developed after the Reformation itself, is the spiritual and theological version of both modernity and modern colonialism.

One could of course argue that Protestant Orthodoxy was staunchly resistant to the spirit of modernity. Certainly the decisions of Dort (1618–19) and Westminster (1643) may be called anything but modern, and the same is true of François Turretin (1623–87) in Geneva. But it is also true that its very opposition to modernity led Protestant Orthodoxy to take upon itself the marks of modernity. To the objective, verifiable, universal, rational truths of modernity, Reformed Orthodoxy opposed the equally objective, verifiable, universal, and even rational truths of the Calvinist gospel—the difference being not so much in methods or in understandings of the nature of truth, as in the first principles on which such truths were founded. Seventeenth-century Protestant Orthodoxy was Reformation theology responding to the early challenges of modernity, and therefore was itself surreptitiously molded by that very modernity that it sought to contradict.

By the nineteenth century, the vast majority of Protestant theologians seemed to believe that Protestantism and modernity went together. In Europe, this led to Protestant liberalism. In the United States, it gave rise to a particular view of the United States and of its place amid the nations of the world. After the Civil War, the nation sought to build its unity on the ideological basis that it had a providential role in humanity's progress. That role was understood institutionally–promoting liberal democracy; religiously–contributing to the spread of Protestantism and its liberties; and racially–in terms of the superiority of the white race, and particularly of its Anglo-Saxon branch. Thus, Josiah Strong, General Secretary of the Evangelical Alliance, affirmed that God was preparing the Anglo-Saxon race, which represented "the largest liberty, the purest Christianity, the highest civilization," for the "final competition of the races," when the Anglo-Saxon race would serve God by "dispossessing the weaker ones, assimilating others, and molding the rest," so that all of humanity would be Anglo-Saxonized.[5] Although Strong represented the conservative wing of Protestant Christianity, similar sentiments were expressed by his liberal counterparts, who felt that the Nordic races were called by God to free the rest of the world from medieval obscurantism and Catholic tyranny.

Although I did not notice it when I first studied that period, today I am fascinated by the manner in which conservative Christians who would consider the theory of evolution an absolute negation of scripture could so flagrantly combine Calvinistic notions of providence with Darwinian ideas of the survival of the fittest.

In any case, the world map presented to me as I grew up was, I am sorry to say, very similar to all this. It did not include the racist overtones of Josiah Strong's statement–at least not overtly. But it certainly did depict the world as moving inexorably toward a future civilization that would be democratic, Protestant, and based on free enterprise. It was a map in which the traditions of the Protestant North Atlantic would soon become the traditions of the entire world. It was a modern world map in which the entire world was moving toward uniformity, based on objective scientific knowledge, and in which differences of cultures, traditions, values, and perspectives were considered temporary aberrations in humanity's irresistible march toward the future.

The Decadence of the Old Map

Today that map has changed and is changing. Some of these changes come from the map's very center, and others from what used to be the periphery.

From inside comes the postmodern criticism of modernity. This criticism in many ways agrees with what comes from the periphery. In this respect, Zygmunt Bauman says the following:

> For most of its history, modernity lived in and through self-deception. Concealment of its own parochiality, conviction that whatever is not universal in its particularity is not-yet-universal, that the project of universality may be incomplete, but remains most definitely on, was the core of that self-deception. It was perhaps thanks to that self-deception that modernity could deliver both the wondrous and the gruesome things it did.[6]

What is happening in Western civilization is, as Jean-François Lyotard has repeatedly argued, the collapse of the master narratives of modernity, the most important of which is that through scientific research and applied technology humankind will be able to develop a society free of the evils of injustice, warfare, and poverty. The reality of events themselves has sufficed to put an end to this grand narrative, showing that its unspoken assumptions were as unwarranted as those of many other metanarratives that modernity dismissed as mere myths.[7] The supposedly objective knowledge of Western modernity is just as conditioned by a particular perspective and a particular set of interests as were many of the previously criticized metanarratives.

From the periphery come new voices—or rather, ancient voices that modernity had smothered. These are, first, the voices of former colonies—places where Western culture and religion came clothed in the trappings of technological and military superiority. A clear phenomenon of recent times is that people in former Western colonies have learned to distinguish between Western technology and all the rest of Western civilization, and are making choices as to what and how much of those to accept or reject. There are also voices of ethnic minorities hitherto suppressed in Western societies: natives of America and other conquered lands; descendants of slaves imported from Africa, or of indentured servants from Asia;

and immigrant minorities in several Western societies. And there are also the voices of women and of the poor, not only in the Third World or among ethnic minorities, but also within the dominant cultures of the West. All these voices are insistently saying, in a myriad of different ways, that what Western modernity took to be objective was in a great measure the objectification of Western male interests and practices; that what modernity took to be universal was also to an extent the imposition of Western ways on the rest of the world; that what modernity took as merely rational was a reflection of a particular way of thinking, no less influenced than others by collective subjective values and perspectives.

These are the voices of those whom modernity excluded–or rather, those whom modernity included not as subjects of their own actions, but rather, as objects to be civilized, controlled, modernized, or, all other euphemisms aside, exploited. They are the voices of those who have much to gain by the demise of modernity–or rather, by its decline, for declaring the demise of modernity may be as premature as was the announcement of Mark Twain's death. (Note that I say "premature," not "false." Mark Twain did die, and so will modernity, even though at this time there are many–the majority–in our society who still live in the illusion that modernity will go on forever.)

These new voices–or rather, these ancient voices that have long been suppressed–have every reason to rejoice when leading voices in the West declare that modernity is on the way out. Now the world map that put us at the periphery will have to be redrawn. Now the metanarrative–or grand myth–of progress, justice, freedom, and peace coming exclusively from the modern North Atlantic no longer holds. Now we are free to draw our own maps, to tell and retell our own metanarratives. And in that we rejoice.

Postmodernity Is Not Enough

Yet there is also reason to be wary. The very name *postmodernity* is still suspiciously modern. It implies that modernity having reached its limits, humankind is now moving to a new stage that is built on the foundations of modernity. Jean-François Lyotard himself practically declares as much at the very beginning of his famous study on *The Postmodern Condition*. He says: "The object of

...udy is the condition of knowledge in the most highly ...eveloped societies. I have decided to use the word postmodern to describe that condition."[8] Note that here again, as in modernity, Lyotard is interested in the state of knowledge only in a certain portion of the world, which he calls "the most highly developed societies." There is much that could be said about this. It implies that the modern metanarrative is still valid, at least on three points that are highly debatable: first, that knowledge, rather than wisdom, is the crux of the matter; second, that knowledge always moves from the center to the periphery; third, that the process whereby a portion of the world has become affluent at the expense of the rest of the world deserves the name of "development"—itself a typically modern and Western notion.

By this I do not mean to discredit either Lyotard or the entire discussion on postmodernity. It is clear that many of those engaged in the discussion of postmodernity, and announcing the passing of modernity, have profound commitments against all forms of imperialism and exploitation, be they economic, political, or cultural. Indeed, much of the postmodern attack on the metanarrative of modernity has been also an attack on the ethnocentrism of that metanarrative.

What I do mean is that there is in postmodernity an ambiguity similar to that of modernity, and that those whom modernity systematically kept at the periphery must be aware of such ambiguities.

Many centuries ago, Irenaeus asserted that the power of a lie resides in the element of truth it contains.[9] Likewise, the power of modernity to convince and convict came from the elements of truth, freedom, and justice that it did produce. Modernity generated much injustice, but it also led to medical discoveries, increased food production, and democratic ideals.[10]

Likewise, when it comes to postmodernity, we must acknowledge the service it renders by unmasking the failings of modernity, particularly its connection with imperialism and exploitation. But at the same time we must be wary of the entanglements of postmodernity with the power systems of modernity.

Let me state it as clearly as I can: When postmoderns speak of the demise of the modern metanarrative, there is reason to rejoice, for the modern metanarrative defined peace, progress, freedom, and justice in ways that were clearly beneficial to its own centers of power and detrimental to the rest of humankind. But when the same voices claim that this means the demise of all metanarratives, we have reason to be leery, for without metanarratives it becomes impossible to speak of such issues as justice, peace, and freedom.

Extramodernity

In this regard, we must remember that besides the modern and the postmodern there is the extramodern—those many voices and perspectives that modernity either ignored or patronized and that postmodernity still patronizes and ignores.

I have stated that as I was growing up, my mental map was essentially a modern map. That is only partly true, for as I was growing up, there was also an alternative map. This was a map developed mostly in church, out of our reading of scripture, out of our worship of the God of scripture, out of the experience of prayer spoken and of prayer answered. It was also a map that resounded with many traditional elements of my own culture. This other map was essentially an extramodern map. It was a map of a world in which God intervened in mysterious yet clear ways. It was a map of a world in which God did free the children of Israel out of the yoke of Egypt, and in which Jesus Christ did indeed rise from the dead. It was a map of a world created by God, sustained by God, directed by God, open to God, and responsible to God even in spite of itself.

Then I became educated—or, what seemed to be the same, I was brought into the modern mind-set. I was told by many books and many teachers that my other map was "pre-critical" and "naive." The world was best understood as a closed system of causes and effects, a very complicated machine in which there was no room for divine intervention. I was taught new, scientific methods for the study of scripture—methods that helped me understand much better how texts had been formed, but gave me no clue what to do with them or what they might mean for me or for my church. I was told that I ought to pray, for prayer was a good devotional exercise, but that I should not really think that God was listening, and much less that God would answer. Church was good, and people should go to church, because church builds character and provides the foundation for a democratic society. What I had learned and believed and practiced earlier must be abandoned because that was fundamentalism, and fundamentalism was the backwoods theology of the Scopes trial. (It took me many years to come to the realization that there was no way I could have been a fundamentalist at that time, because fundamentalism is a modern reaction to modernity, and the faith that we lived in our churches was in reality extramodern.)

Something similar happened with my involvement in the problems of society and my attempts to deal with them. Even before I was born, my father had been a revolutionary activist, partly on the premise that God would change things and that it was best to be on the side of God. My modern education told me that political and social systems are just as closed to divine intervention as the rest of the world. The future will evolve of what is here now. There is no reason to expect discontinuities, radical revolutions in which something comes out of what was not. Therefore, modern Christians should only embrace causes for which they see a hope of success—which generally meant relatively moderate and tame causes. Gone was the God who freed Israel out of the yoke of Egypt. Gone was the God who raised Jesus Christ from among the dead. Gone was the God who would intervene on behalf of my country and my people.

Still, I never completely abandoned that earlier map. In more recent years, I have slowly come to the realization that modernity itself is a worldview just as mythical as any other, with no particular claim except that it has been promoted by the most powerful people in the world and has enjoyed a measure of success in some rather limited spheres—of which the most notable is technology. I have also come to realize that there is nothing particularly irrational, or backward, or barbaric in being extramodern. Indeed, it is now clear that in spite of all the propaganda of modernity, most of the world is still as extramodern as I was in my earlier days. Still, I am a product of modernity, and as such I often find myself leading the strange life of a traveler who has a different map in each of two pockets, and who never knows which of the two to follow.

Furthermore, this tension between two different and even contradictory intellectual maps, or in more technical terms, between two metanarratives, is not my experience alone. It is also the experience of most of what in this country we have come to know by the strangely contradictory term of "mainline Christianity." At bottom, the malaise in our denominations comes from our refusal to recognize, and our inability to live with, the tension between two metanarratives, one that places us at the very heart of modernity, and another that at many points is incompatible with modernity.

Meanwhile, particularly among those whom modernity has excluded, the church has been growing, to the point that today most Christians are not white and do not live in the North Atlantic. As long as the world map of modernity held sway, these Christians seemed to have little to say of theological significance. Today, as we begin to glimpse the demise of modernity and the beginning of a new era, it may be that the renewal of theology, and indeed the renewal of our church life, will come at least in part from those branches of the church that have long been excluded from the "benefits" of modernity.

5

Mapping a New Catholicity

In the previous chapter I discussed how our map of the
intellectual world has changed as we move from modernity to
postmodernity. The next task is to begin exploring what that might
mean for Christian theology. Before doing that, however, it is
important to take a moment to reflect on the similarities between
our age and that in which Christianity was born and shaped.

If it is true that our map of the world has changed drastically,
it is also true that the map of the world had changed, and was still
changing, at the time around the birth of Christianity.

Changing Maps in Antiquity and Today

The world map of Socrates and his Athenian contemporaries
was composed of two concentric circles. First, and most
importantly, the inner circle was Athens and her dependencies.
Then there was an outer circle that included Sparta and all of
Greece, Ionia, and even Magna Graecia. Beyond that second circl'
was the amorphous and intellectually unimportant mass '
"barbarians," who only were important when, as in the case

the Persian Wars, they became a threat to Greece. When Plato proposed the ideal state, he was not speaking, as we tend to think today, of a nation with millions of inhabitants stretching for hundreds of miles in each direction. He was thinking in terms of the Greek polis and how its government could be perfected. His disciple Aristotle made it very clear that there was a significant, primal difference between Greeks and barbarians, in that all barbarians are by nature slaves:

> There is no natural ruler among them: they are a community of slaves, male and female. Wherefore the poets say, It is meet that Hellenes should rule over barbarians; as if they thought that the barbarian and the slave were by nature one.[1]

In this sense, the world map of the ancient Greek was very much like the world map of the early modern European. Here too there were two concentric circles: first the nation, then the rest of "civilization." The remainder, beyond that second circle, was the amorphous and intellectually unimportant mass of "the heathen."

In ancient times, change was brought about primarily by one of Aristotle's disciples, Alexander of Macedonia. If it is true, as Aristotle said, that the highest form of civilization is the Greek and that the rest are by nature slaves, it follows that the task of a Greek ruler is to make that truth effective. Hence the ideological justification for Alexander's conquests. Imperialism seldom sees itself as a crass grab for power and privilege. In the case of Alexander, his conquests had a civilizing intent: to bring to all the benefits of Greek culture, which all those barbarians so sadly lacked. If the process also deprived them of their national independence and turned many of them into something like slaves, that was simply their natural state, and thus a most appropriate condition for them.

But Alexander was more than a philosopher. He was also a shrewd politician who was willing to respect and even assimilate the customs of some of these barbarians, as long as it helped him toward his ultimate goal. In Egypt he presented himself as the deliverer from Persian tyranny. He offered sacrifices to the Egyptian god Apis, took the double crown of the pharaohs, and

showed great respect for the religious leadership and the traditions of the land. In Persia he attempted the same policy, though with less success. Thus, while his imperial ventures were based on an ideology of strict, natural superiority on the part of all that was Greek, the realities of politics led to an encounter and intermingling of cultures that was not simply unidirectional.

Significantly, and partly as a result of such widening horizons, another of Aristotle's disciples, Theophrastus, argued that all humans are related, and suggested the possibility of a common ancestry for all of humanity.[2] By the beginning of the second century B.C.E., Eratosthenes was declaring that people ought not to be classified as Greeks or barbarians, but as good or evil.[3]

Here again we may see a parallelism with what took place at the beginning of the modern era. The map that centered on the North Atlantic, and that saw the rest of the world as heathendom, led to the notion of the white man's burden, which provided the ideological justification for the British and several other European empires. On this side of the Atlantic, the doctrine of "manifest destiny" led to similar imperial expansion. Political and economic colonialism was one of the results of this shifting map. Christian missions and the rise of the so-called "younger churches" were another result.

Alexander's map was short-lived, not only because his empire crumbled immediately after his death but also because the cultures and traditions that were at first overwhelmed by Hellenism soon began to give signs of new life. Scholars often distinguish between two stages within Hellenism. The first is the stage in which Greek culture seemed to overwhelm the known world. Almost overnight, Greek became the language of the cultured elites throughout that world. Ancient cultural differences seemed to disappear. As one scholar has put it, "The most striking feature of the Hellenistic world as compared with what went before is its approximation to uniformity in the daily habits and outward surroundings of life."[4] He then goes on to say that "of the peoples newly subjected to hellenization it may be said that they welcomed the innovations, despite, or it may be because of, the fact that they themselves were heirs to venerable civilizations."[5]

Eventually, however, the reaction set in. There was a resurgence of ancient cultures and religions, often as a means of resistance against Hellenistic influences. In many cases—Egypt, Judea, Persia—the resistance took the form of open and sometimes successful revolt. The story of the Maccabean rebellion, and later of the Jewish wars against Rome, is well known. In Egypt there was an equally prolonged history of riots, revolts, and rebellions that began at approximately the same time as the Christian era. In 122 C.E. a major riot in Alexandria led Emperor Hadrian to modify some of his policies. Thirty years later, another rebellion took more than a year to quench. And again twenty years after that. And again and again a dozen times during the next century. However, such revolts were not against Hellenism per se, or against everything Hellenistic. They were, rather, against the suppression of certain elements of traditional culture and against the exploitation of those of more ancient stock by the new arrivals— be they Greek or Roman. That is why at various points and stages of its development the Maccabean revolt may be seen as a reaction against Hellenism, and at other points as supporting it. And the same is true of rebellion in Egypt and in Persia. Thus, in concluding his far-reaching study of Near Eastern resistance to Hellenism, Samuel K. Eddy remarks:

> In the final analysis Oriental resistance was an effort to maintain a native way of life whose continuity was threatened by Hellenism. The reaction was directed only at those Greek institutions which were actually in action against Oriental institutions. There was no opposition to Hellenism in its totality, and there was no effort made by anybody to destroy Hellenism entirely. One does not find hatred expressed in the literature against the rationality of Hellenism, or its scientific or philosophical achievements.[6]

Thus, it seems appropriate to summarize the Hellenistic age by dividing it, as Hans Jonas does, into two distinct periods:

> the period of manifest Greek dominance and oriental submersion, and the period of reaction of a renascent East, which in its turn advanced victoriously in a kind of spiritual counterattack into the West and reshaped the universal culture.[7]

In this too we can see a parallelism with the way the map of the world has evolved during the modern age. For a time, the West overwhelmed the rest of the world. Difficult as it may be for us to believe today, this was not always done against the will of those whose ancient cultures were overwhelmed by early colonialism. In Latin America, liberal elements who feared the conservatism of Spain and its traditions welcomed and sometimes, in fact, invited North American and British economic and even military intervention. In Africa, Madagascar, and many of the islands of the Pacific, local rulers welcomed Westerners as allies against traditional enemies, eventually to find that both they and their enemies had been engulfed by Western colonialism. Japan resisted Western penetration until forced to open its doors by American naval might. But once it had become open to Western influences, it took the lead in accommodating such influences, in the hope of outmodernizing the West.

Thus developed the first stage of Western modern influence throughout the world, in many ways parallel to the first stage of the Hellenistic era. As Kenneth Scott Latourette put it in his massive review of the history of Christian missions,

> Out of the world-wide expansion of Europe and the transformation of non-European cultures through contact with the West came a…feature of the nineteenth century–the beginning of a world culture. This world culture was really an extension of the civilization of Europe. The most prominent characteristics of the cosmopolitan culture were the most obvious features of nineteenth century Europe–the machine, the products of the machine, and the types of education which enabled men [sic] to build and operate machines.[8]

That was the first stage. Then came a second stage, parallel to Hans Jonas' second division of the Hellenistic era. This is the stage of revival of cultures and traditions that had long been suppressed by Western influence and that many had expected to wither and die. It is this second stage in which we are living, as I tried to show in the previous chapter.

The second stage of Hellenism was the time of resurgence of traditions that had seemed to disappear under the weight of Greek ideas and political dominance. An important element in that second stage was a revival of many of the ancient Eastern religions. Even before the time of Caesar, that is, before the advent of Christianity, two of these religions had begun the process of revitalization: Jewish Yahwism and Parthian Mazdaism or Zoroastrianism. The latter was successful to the point that it gave rise to a new Parthian empire. The Yahwist revival was not as successful politically, leading eventually to the fall of Jerusalem and the siege and tragedy of Masada. But it was successful both in creating a renewal of commitment to the ancient faith in Judea and in producing the sort of Yahwism represented by Philo and others—a Yahwism that soon found itself making its defense before Hellenistic culture and making converts from among that culture. Similarly, though in most cases at a slightly later date, other ancient religions enjoyed their own revivals, including the cult of Isis and Osiris in Egypt, Babylonian astrology, the Magna Mater of Asia, the ancient mysteries of Thracia, and many others. In that revival, however, these ancient religions presented themselves under a new garb—one that had been influenced by Hellenism and most particularly by its cosmopolitan perspectives. Thus, Mazdaism was reborn, not only as a religion of and for the Parthians and their closest neighbors but also as a worldview that soon began to make an impact throughout the Mediterranean basin. Isis and Osiris now became not only a religion for Egyptians of the higher classes but a religion into which people from all sorts of different cultural and social backgrounds could be initiated. One could likewise argue that Christianity, as an offshoot of Yahwism, differed from its mother religion in ways similar to those in which each of these newer versions of ancient religions differed from earlier versions. Christianity, like most of those new versions of old religions, broke the ethnic boundaries of the ancient religion, no longer connecting national origin with religious affiliation, and emphasizing instead personal decision and initiation.

Be that as it may, what is undeniable is that at the time of the birth of Christianity, there were in the ancient Hellenistic world, and indeed throughout the Roman Empire, a number of religions, most of them Eastern in origin, vying for the commitment of people. As is well known and as every textbook on church history points out, most of these religions were syncretistic, allowing admixtures from other religions, and even allowing people to belong to more than one at the same time.

As is also well known, these syncretistic tendencies were among the greatest challenges that the early church had to face, particularly since there were those who sought to combine Christianity with various ancient beliefs. Most notable among these were the various gnostic teachers and schools, some of which combined the name of Jesus and the message of the cross with Babylonian astrology, Zoroastrian dualism, and other assorted teachings. In response to such challenges, we have repeatedly been told–and I myself have repeatedly said–the early church developed such instruments as the canon of the New Testament, the doctrine of apostolic succession, and the various creeds.

The parallelisms between the last centuries of Hellenism and these last decades of modernity are striking, particularly in religious matters. Toward the end of Hellenism, the ancient centers of Greek culture were being invaded by a wide variety of religious perspectives from the previously subdued East. Today, toward the end of modernity, the traditional centers of Western culture are being invaded–successfully invaded, I should say–by a similar variety of religious views from previously subdued and suppressed cultures–religious views that at the height of modernity seemed to be on the way toward extinction. This includes not only ancient religions such as Buddhism, Islam, and Hinduism in their traditional garb but also all sorts of newly created, Westernized versions of those religions, as well as witches' covens, spiritualist seances, *botánicas de santería,* crystals imbued with supernatural power, and many others.

Sectarianism and Syncretism

It has often been said that the main theological challenge that the early church had to face was the threat of syncretism–the danger that Christianity would be reduced to the status of one more ingredient in the spiritual melting pot of the times. It has also been said, and I think quite correctly, that we today face a similar challenge.

What is often missed, however, is that syncretism and sectarianism often go hand in hand, that it is possible to use the threat of syncretism as an excuse for sectarianism, and that even syncretism can be sectarian. As its name implies, a sect is a group that takes its own sector of reality and experience for the whole. The term *sect* does not in itself say anything about the truth or falsehood, the orthodoxy or heterodoxy, of the group's teachings. What it actually says is that the group, no matter how orthodox, errs in that it considers its own sector of reality, its own limited perspective, to be the whole of reality, or the only allowable perspective. A sect may be perfectly orthodox. Indeed, it may be more orthodox than anyone else. But inasmuch as it considers itself to be the only possible orthodoxy, it is sectarian.

In this regard, the challenge of the gnostic teachers was not only in their syncretism. It was also in their sectarianism. Likewise, Marcion claimed to be the only true interpreter of Paul and his message—and by implication turned Paul himself into a sectarian, whose disagreement with Peter and the rest implied that they had no idea what the gospel was all about, whereas he did. Various gnostic teachers each claimed to have a secret tradition given by Jesus to a particular apostle and then passed on to them; or they claimed to have a single book in which the entire truth was written, a gospel of Peter, or of Thomas, or of James, or of Truth. Thus, the problem was not only that these gnostic believers mixed Christianity with all sorts of ingredients foreign to it but also that they claimed that their mixture was *the* true formula.

It is for this reason that when the early church sought for a word to describe such doctrines, it spoke of them not only as heterodox but also as "heretical." Like *sectarian,* the word *heretical* in and of itself originally did not refer primarily to the orthodoxy or heterodoxy of a group, but rather to its partisanship, to its claim to a hold on truth that is total and unique.

On the other hand, although heterodoxy and sectarianism are in themselves distinct, this does not make the latter any less serious than the former. On the contrary, heterodoxy and sectarianism belong together, for if nothing else, a sect is by definition heterodox in its ecclesiology. Hence, the rapid evolution of the meaning of the word *heresy,* coming to signify, as it does today, doctrinal error.

Universality and Catholicity Are Not the Same

As the early church sought for a word to describe itself in opposition both to syncretism and to sectarianism, it very early settled on the term *catholic*. We are so accustomed to translating the word *catholic* as "universal" that we no longer think about it. Indeed, for many of us the term means simply that the church is one, extended throughout all the world and all the generations. In this, we tend to agree with seventeenth-century Reformed divine John Henry Heidegger, who explained the meaning of "catholicity" by saying simply that "it is the same as 'one,' except that it denotes the extension of the unity."[9]

But in fact catholicity means much more than that.[10] Etymologically, it means "according to the whole," and thus is not exactly the same as either "universal" or "one." "Universal" is that which is uniformly present everywhere; "cath'holic" is that which is according to the whole, that in which all have a place. Sometimes the two can have similar meanings, but sometimes they can be diametrically opposed. Suppose, for instance, that Alexander had been able to conquer the entire world. In that case his rule would have been universal, but it would not have been cath'holic. Or, taking another example from early Christian literature, in an often quoted passage[11] Irenaeus says that there are "four catholic winds." Modern translators say "four universal winds." But the fact is that were the North wind to become the only wind, it would be universal, but it would no longer be cath'holic. What makes the wind cath'holic is the fact that there is a North wind, and a South wind, and an East wind, and a West wind, and all together make this cath'holic movement of the atmosphere.

With that in mind, let us look as the main instruments that the early church employed as a response both to syncretism and to sectarianism: the canon of the New Testament, the authority of the episcopacy, and the Creed.

When putting together the four gospels in our present canon, the church insisted that this was the cath'holic witness to the gospel, not only in the sense that it was orthodox, or that it was believed everywhere, but also in the sense that it was the witness of the whole. It was cath'holic in the sense that it was not partial, nor sectarian, nor even the witness of a single apostle. It was cath'holic in the sense that it was *katà Mathàion,* according to Matthew; *and katà Márkon,* according to Mark; *and* according to Luke; *and* according to John, even though Matthew, Mark, Luke, and John did not agree on a number of matters—or, I would even venture to say, precisely because they were different! The multiform witness to a single gospel was more credible, more universal in the catholic sense, precisely because it was multiform.

Thus, the canon is a response not only to the syncretism that threatened the church, but also to the sectarianism that was an equally serious threat. The church cath'holic is a church that, while being one, includes within its canon the cath'holic multiform witness of the four gospels, as well as the cath'holic multiform witness of its many different members and constituencies.

This leads us to the second instrument that the early church–often called "the old cath'holic church"–employed in its response to syncretism and sectarianism: episcopal authority. It has often been pointed out that the doctrine of apostolic succession emerged as a response to the threat of heresy. What we often forget is that apostolic succession, like the canon, was a move both for closure and for openness. Apostolic succession certainly meant that new teachers could not invent new doctrines unless, as Tertullian ironically said, they can prove "that Christ has come a second time, has been present and teaching a second time, crucified a second time, dead a second time, raised a second time."[12] But it also meant that any doctrine that claimed to have come down from a particular apostle had to be judged by the testimony of all the bishops of all the churches who had received their commission from all the apostles.[13] In this again, early Christian writers were aware that there were differences from place to place and from church to church. Yet this church, with its various regional particularities, was the church cath'holic. Hence the insistence of Cyprian (in the third century) on episcopal collegiality, so that while there is only one episcopacy, each bishop represents the whole of it,[14] and they each manage their affairs according to their own local customs.[15] Thus, in its original form, the church's insistence on apostolic succession is another way to ensure its cath'holicity, both against various forms of syncretism and against the sectarianism of some–in the case of Cyprian, the sectarian tendencies of the bishop of Rome.

Third, the Creed is often mentioned along with the canon and with apostolic succession as means whereby the early cath'holic church responded to the challenge of heresy. In this regard, two points must be made: first, the early creeds were minimalist; and second, they were usually local or at best regional. By calling them "minimalist," I mean that the early creeds did not seek to summarize all of Christian doctrine. Rather, to the basic Trinitarian structure that they derived from their baptismal origins the creeds added whatever was necessary to counteract the errors that they addressed. Thus, the Old Roman Symbol, the predecessor of our Apostles' Creed, sought to respond to Marcionite and gnostic doctrines, and for that reason emphasized the christological clause. Likewise, the Nicene is clearly written in response to and refutation of Arianism. By "local," I mean that most creeds were used only in a particular city or region, and that in early times there was no requirement that all churches use the same creed. That was the reason why, even after the promulgation of the Creed of Nicea, many churches continued using different creeds, and it took generations for the Niceno-Constantinopolitan Creed to become the most commonly used throughout Christendom. Thus, creeds were not intended to universalize doctrine, but rather, to build specific responses to the challenges of a time or a place on the foundational Trinitarian doctrine and the baptismal experience.

Catholicity, Postmodernity, and Extramodernity

If we now join all of this with what has been said earlier about the changing world map of postmodernity, and more specifically about the changing world map of the church, the implications are far-reaching. Just as modernity brought about an enormous expansion of Western influence, it also brought about an unprecedented missionary movement, so that, as Archbishop Temple so aptly put it, for the first time the church of Christ became truly universal. And just as the decline of modernity has brought about the end of colonialism and a resurgence of ancient, previously suppressed cultures and traditions, it has also brought about the emergence of new perspectives on the gospel from every corner of the earth.

Clearly, the dangers of this emerging situation are many. First and most obviously, there is always the danger of syncretism—the danger that we may be so open to all sorts of influences that we may lose the very heart of the gospel. The danger is very real, but so much has been said and is still being said about it that I see no need to expand on that point here.

The other danger is more insidious, because it is less apparent. It is the danger of sectarianism; the danger that we might come to confuse the Western interpretation of the gospel with the gospel itself; the danger that, by insisting that our own theological outlook must be universally accepted, we cease being cath'holic.

The reason that entire sections of the church today ignore the challenge of true catholicity is that the modern intellectual map makes it difficult to be truly catholic. By insisting on objectivity, the modern map makes no allowance for the importance of perspective in all knowledge—including theological and religious knowledge. By insisting on universality, it invites each particular perspective to impose itself on the rest—in other words, it invites every theology and every tradition to become sectarian.

In these last days of modernity, as the map of the world changes drastically and so does the map of worldwide Christianity, what does it mean to be a church cath'holic? It certainly means, as many of the more conservative critics of Third World theologies have repeatedly pointed out, that we must guard against the dangers of syncretism. There is indeed in some circles a tendency to theological faddism, in which the main premise seems to be that if something is new and unheard of, it must be true—at least for the time being! In this respect our times are quite similar to the early times of the church, when some people set out to collect bits of wisdom and religion from all sorts of different sources, and to experiment as much as possible with the enormous variety of options offered. And we do well to remember that second-century novel *Metamorphoses* of Lucius Apuleius, whose hero pays for his insatiable curiosity and religious fickleness by becoming an ass—a golden ass, yes, but asinine nevertheless.

Against the syncretism of the gnostics, as well as against any other form of syncretism that challenged the core of the Christian faith, the early church developed what is still the most potent weapon: the canon of scripture. If there is danger of syncretism in today's church, our most sure recourse is to the word of God, by which every doctrine and tradition must be measured.

But if there is the Scylla of syncretism, there is also the Charybdis of sectarianism—a danger against which many in the Western church have not been sufficiently vigilant.

Hidden Sectarianism

It is true that "mainline" denominations in general have been aware of the danger of sectarianism as it works in our society and within our milieu. But there are other forms of sectarianism that, although less evident, are no less real and no less insidious.

First, there is what I would call North Atlantic sectarianism, for lack of a better term. This is the sectarianism that tempts the former center of the modern world to believe that its own perspectives and traditions are still normative, even in the emerging postmodern, polycentric world. This type of sectarianism is quite prevalent among our mainline denominations in this country. And it is all the more prevalent because there is a measure of justification for it in that North Atlantic theology in the last few centuries has provided the entire church with significant insights into the meaning of the gospel. Yet in spite of such partial justification, to continue this day with essentially the same theological curricula as fifty years ago; to offer course bibliographies in which everything is originally written in English, German, or Dutch; to ignore the theological insights of those who are writing and teaching in Japanese, Swahili, Spanish, or Quiché in these days of the closing of modernity cannot be called anything but sectarian.

Then there is socioeconomic sectarianism. This is the sectarianism that I find most prevalent in the theological circles of my own denomination and of many other so-called mainline denominations. This is the sectarianism of my friend who insisted that in order to be a full participant in his denomination, one has to be born into it. It is the sectarianism of those who seem to think that to be a Christian one has to be sophisticated, according to Western, middle-class canons of sophistication. It is the sectarianism of those in our mainline denominations who apparently believe that nothing good can come out of the Nazareths of our ghettos and barrios. If I may put it quite bluntly, it is the sectarianism that does not see the contradiction of a church, in a society in which so many are increasingly marginalized, calling itself at the same time "mainline" and "Christian."

If to be sectarian means to stake a sector of reality and take it for the whole, then sectarianism may well be the greatest danger facing the North Atlantic mainline denominations today.

The Canon as a Paradigm of Catholicity

How are we to respond to that challenge, to guard against that danger? Perhaps here again we may profit from the example of the early church, and especially from that most precious heritage it has left us, the canon of scripture. Or to put it in traditional Reformed terms, by being not only *ecclesia reformata* but also *ecclesia reformanda* **according to the Word of God**. And by remembering that the canon of the written word is itself a cath'holic canon. By including four *different* gospels in its canon, as a multiform witness to the single gospel of Jesus Christ, the early church, the early cath'holic church, taught us what postmodernity is also saying: perspective is always a part of truth—at least of truth as seen from the human side.[16] Marcion the sectarian may be content with the single witness of Luke and claim that the gospel of Luke is the true, the only true, interpretation of the life and work of Jesus. But the church cath'holic insists that the gospel of Luke, in order to be cath'holic, must be placed together with Matthew, Mark, and John. These four all read the same Hebrew Scriptures, all witnessed to the same Jesus. Yet they are different. And precisely because they are different, all four are necessary for the cath'holicity of the canon.

Even though this multiplicity of perspectives may seem to our modern mentality to obscure or even deny the truth of the gospel, in fact the opposite is the case. If in a trial all witnesses agree on every detail, down to the last word, their testimony is not credible, for they must have been rehearsed. The value and credibility of such witnesses depend on their giving testimony to the same central event, even though seeing it and interpreting it in various ways. Likewise, the quadriform witness to the gospel, even though sometimes puzzling to our modern, objectifying frame of mind, is in fact more credible than a single, uniform witness.

Furthermore, what is true of the gospels is also true of the entire Bible. Thus, from the very first chapters of Genesis we have at least two accounts of creation. These accounts differ on matters such as the order in which things are created—in one, animals are created first, and then humans, male and female, while in the other, the man is created first, then the animals, and finally the woman. Those who today claim that they take the Genesis story of creation literally, in fact do not follow any one of the two accounts, but rather a compilation of elements from both, and are therefore baffled when faced with the actual text of Genesis. A truly literal reading of Genesis forces us to a cath'holic view of creation—one that does not fall into the sectarian option of choosing one particular account over the other. The same is true not only of the stories of creation but of the rest of the canon of scripture, where the views of the prophets often differ from the views of the priests, and where Paul interprets the gospel one way, and John in another way.

What this means is that the written word of God, by its very structure and composition, calls us also to cath'holicity, to listen to what other interpreters from other perspectives find in the text and in the story. This requires a structure and a self-understanding that, like the canon of the New Testament, can bind the irreducible contributions of various perspectives in an indissoluble unity.

Much to its credit, the church has repeatedly rejected the temptation to reduce the four gospels into one, to solve the difficulties by merging the four into a single story. In that, it has been true to its cath'holic tradition, and to the cath'holic intent of the canon.

It is important to realize that the impulse to have a single gospel is parallel to the sectarian impulse. We would like to have a single gospel because then all questions would be answered unequivocally: we would know exactly how many people Jesus fed, with how many fish and how many loaves, and we would no longer have to fear contradiction within the word of God. The problem is that when the word of God no longer contradicts us, it risks being confused with our own words. Likewise, the sectarian impulse seeks to have a single, clearly identifiable body that holds all truth and that therefore has nothing to learn from others. Therefore, most sects have dreams and hopes of becoming universal, of encompassing the whole world; but no sect is ready to become cath'holic, to embrace a multitude of perspectives from various parts of the body of Christ.

The sectarian impulse is parallel to the modern claim of objectivity and universality. Just as modernity dreamed of a single world map with a single culture, so do sectarians dream of a single theology, a single doctrine, a single gospel—or at least a single reading of all four gospels.

This is the same impulse that progressively eroded the collegial authority of the episcopacy, turning it into a hierarchy, and eventually leading to the decision that the head of that hierarchy is infallible. A church conceived in the terms of the Council of Trent and of the First Vatican Council may be universal, but it certainly is not cath'holic!

At this point one may add that the vast difference between Vatican I and Vatican II was not due only to the difference between Pius IX and John XXIII, great as that difference was. It was also due to the difference in the composition of the two councils. Commenting on his own experience at the second of these councils, Father Thomas Stransky says that by the third session

> It was becoming clear that the Roman Catholic Church is no longer a Mediterranean church, as it was in the first eight councils; no more a West-European church, as it appeared during the Middle Ages; nor a South-European church as it seemed at the Council of Trent; and no more a world-wide church governed by European bishops, as it was at Vatican I. Vatican II became the first council in which Europe—if we think of Europe reaching into the Levant—had not the predominant voice. With one-fifth of the episcopate coming from Latin-America and over one-third from the churches of Asia, Africa and Oceania, and with a surprisingly articulate unanimity among these bishops, the first two sessions marked the transition of the Church from a European basis to a world-wide one.

And then, in a sentence that resonates with what I have been arguing about the full meaning of cath'holicity, Stransky concludes:

> For the first time in its history, the Church had to face up to the full implications of its catholicity.[17]

Sectarianism has other dimensions than those we usually take into consideration. Sectarianism may be connected with geography, with culture, and with class. The words of Father Stransky regarding the changes that took place around the Second Vatican Council may be read as a confession of an earlier geographic sectarianism on the part of Roman Catholicism. Impelled by the changing world map, the Roman Catholic Church had to face the reality of its own geographic and cultural sectarianism and take up the challenge of becoming more truly cath'holic.

Other churches have gone through a similar process. In this respect, the history of the World Council of Churches, and the various streams of ecumenism that have come to converge in it, is illustrative. The trend is well known. At the World Missionary Conference held in Edinburgh in 1910, out of some twelve hundred participants, seventeen were members of the younger churches. Not one of them, however, represented such a church. (Fourteen were appointed by the missionary agencies with which their churches were connected, and three received personal invitations from the committees planning the conference.) By the time the World Council of Churches met in Vancouver in 1983 there were more member churches in Africa than in Western Europe or in North America. Indeed, all the West European member churches plus all the North American amounted to less than one third of all the member churches of the WCC.

At this point it may be helpful to return to the image of changing world maps. The changes that are taking place in our day are more drastic than those that took place with the Germanic invasions, the advance of Islam, or the Iberian conquest of America. The change is not just the drawing of a new map, but the emergence of a multitude of maps that cannot be reduced into one—much as the four gospels cannot be merged into one.

PART II

The Changing History of Church History

6

The Struggle over the History of Israel

Too often we look upon history as if it were something already done, much as we look at an old building, to which a few new stories may be added with the passing of centuries. In such cases, we are forgetting that church history is itself a theological discipline, and that as such it reflects the theological stances of historians. Precisely because it is a theological discipline, the history of the church has to be corrected constantly as new problems arise, or as the past is read from new perspectives or with new questions in mind.

Furthermore, it is possible to read some of the crucial moments in the history of the church as struggles over the reading of previous history and over who was the true heir of that history. Thus, for instance, when we read Paul's epistles, as well as the entire New Testament, we see there the record of a profound conflict between those Jews who had embraced Christianity and those who rejected it, and the crucial question in that conflict was who had the right to claim the scriptures and inheritance of Israel. When centuries later we come to the controversy between Augustine and the

Pelagians, it is important to remember that part of what was at stake was the question of who had the right to claim the inheritance of Paul and of the rest of the New Testament, and therefore also indirectly to claim the Hebrew tradition. (One must not forget that Pelagius was himself a careful commentator on Paul's epistle to the Romans.) Still later, during the Protestant Reformation, part of what was at stake was the determination of who were the true heirs of Augustine, and therefore of Paul, and therefore of the Hebrew tradition.

As heirs of that entire history, we today quite often forget that what we have actually inherited is the result of all these struggles, and that what today seems settled was once very much debated. Thus, we take it for granted that the best way to read Augustine is through Luther and Calvin, that the best way to read Paul is through Augustine, and that the best way to read the Old Testament is through Paul. When we so do, history narrows our horizons rather than widening them; rather than fostering openness toward other interpretations of scripture and of reality, it impedes it; rather than encouraging ecumenical dialogue, it hinders it.

What all this means is that we have to recognize that history itself has a history. Therefore, it seems best to start our consideration of the manner in which we read history by a brief overview of the earlier history of history.

The Beginnings of History

Some thirty-two centuries before Christ, the Egyptians began recording their history, or at least trying to set up reminders of the victories of their rulers, so that they would be known by later generations. By the period of the fifth dynasty—that is, about the year 2500 B.C.E.—there were writings telling the history of Egypt from its early beginnings.

In Mesopotamia, the Sumerians and the Acadians had theological reasons for keeping historical records. Since they believed that events such as floods, plagues, wars, and the like were due to the will of the gods, and since that will was supposedly known by astrology and could be impacted by the conduct of the rulers and the people, it was important to have records indicating the position of the heavenly bodies and the actions of the people and its rulers whenever an important event took place.

More than a thousand years before Christ, a Phoenician wrote a *Phoenician History,* which was later translated into Greek by Herenius Philo from Byblos. Unfortunately, both the original Phoenician text and the Greek translation have been lost.

In the Western Hemisphere, scholars used to think that the original inhabitants did not have much of a sense of history and that their writings that had remained were mostly astronomical calculations and data. Now, as scholars have begun to decipher and to study Mayan inscriptions, we begin to discover that the supposedly astronomical texts are often historical records: they tell the deeds of kings and dynasties, and they record wars and other similar events.

Among the Greeks, though others before Herodotus of Halicarnassus collected chronological data, as well as myths, about the origins of the people and the sayings of sages, it is he who is properly given the title of "father of history." Herodotus hailed from Ionia, which was also the place where many of the most important presocratic philosophers flourished. What marked that great intellectual awakening in Ionia was its interest in finding an explanation for things that would not be satisfied with the mythical, but were instead based on a logical understanding of reality. That is also one of the characteristics of the *Nine Books of History* of Herodotus. He still includes myths and legends, but he is not as interested in them as he is in the facts and traditions that "seem to be verifiable, or at least believable." That may be seen in the very use of the word *history* to refer to this enterprise.

At that time, the meaning of the word *history* was similar to what today we understand as *research,* that is, a careful review of the data in order to know something. Furthermore, the verb that could be translated as "historify" was commonly used in the sense of visiting someone to get to know that person better. Thus, in Galatians 1:18, where according to the NRSV Paul says he went to Jerusalem "to visit Cephas," what the Greek actually says is that he went there to "historify Cephas." And in Acts 17:23, where the NRSV has Paul saying "I went through the city and looked carefully at the objects of your worship," what the Greek actually says is "I went to the city and historified the objects of your worship."

Therefore, when Herodotus refers to his own work as "history," what he is underscoring is not so much the narrative character of that work as its scientific nature. Certainly, according to today's historiographic canons, Herodotus leaves much to be desired. But even so, his purpose is to produce a narrative based on the analysis of the data and on the most credible witnesses and sources.

If to "historify" was to visit in order to know, Herodotus was certainly a historian. The wide range of his travels is almost incredible, given the conditions of his time. Born in Ionia under Persian rule, he traveled throughout the eastern Mediterranean basin and as far west as Italy; he went into the heartland of Persia; he visited Egypt and then went up the Nile as far as the falls in Elephantine; and he lived among the Scythians to the northeast of Greece. Everywhere he went he took notes. As a result, he deserves to be considered the father not only of history but also of anthropology, of ethnography, and even of the comparative study of religions.

But enough about Herodotus. The important point to be made is that, as was also the case in so many other fields, the Greeks set the pace for what history was to be for several centuries. It was also in Greece that Thucydides wrote about the Peloponnesian wars—wars that began when Herodotus was still alive. Thucydides was then followed by Xenophanes, Polybius, and many others.

Like all the other peoples already mentioned, the Romans sought to preserve the memory of their origins. Cicero says that from a very ancient time it was customary for the high priest to write down important events as they took place, and to exhibit this record in a public place so all could read it. At the end of the year, all that had been written was transferred to a more permanent form, and a new register was begun. This is the origin of the term "annals," that is, annual registers.

When the Roman republic produced its first historians, they had already been influenced by Greek culture to the point that they actually wrote in Greek. The first to write in Latin was Marcus Porcius Cato, also known as "Cato the Elder," whose seven books of *Origins* have been lost. It seems that he tried to imitate Herodotus and the Greek historians. He was then followed by other better known authors, such as Julius Caesar, Sallust, Titus Livy, and many others, leading to those who were practically contemporaries with the New Testament: Tacitus, Suetonius, and the Jewish historian Flavius Josephus.

All this indicates that when the Christian faith first appeared in the Greco-Roman world, and when Christians began to tell their history, they already had abundant antecedents in all the surrounding cultures, especially in the Greek and Roman civilization, in which the first missionary enterprise took place. Therefore, one of the main theological issues that Christians had to face was the relationship between that prolonged history of humankind and the message of the gospel. To this we shall return in chapter 7.

The Judeo-Christian View of History

If I have not mentioned the Jews up to this point, it is precisely because in this "history of Christian history" the Hebrew people deserve special attention. This is not the place to discuss matters such as the historiographic methods employed in the historical books of the Old Testament, their sources, and so on. All of that is carefully studied in many books and courses about the Hebrew Scriptures, and there is no need to review it here.

Two points, however, must be underlined in order to understand how the early Christians understood and wrote their history.

The first point is that the authors of the Old Testament did not write history with the sole purpose of leaving a record of events. Their history had a theological function and a theological perspective. Its purpose was to tell about the relationships of God with the whole of creation, and most specifically with the people of Israel, and to use that narrative as a guide for present and future audiences. In other words, history had a religious and didactic function. The people wrote down their history in order to know how they were to serve their God.

On this point, the history of Israel is not all that different from that of the surrounding nations. The Babylonians kept historical records in order to know how to serve the gods and thus have good harvests and avoid plagues, inundations, and other disasters. Herodotus wrote his history in order to show that Greek democracy was superior to the autocratic government of Persia, and to call his readers to follow the values of the great leaders of the Persian wars. The Egyptians wrote their inscriptions in order to reaffirm the divine character of their rulers, and thus to promote an attitude of obedience toward them as well as toward the entire social order. Therefore, there is little new or different in the fact that among the Hebrews someone wrote, for instance, a book of Judges, which repeatedly affirms that when the people do what is evil before the eyes of God, God turns them over to foreign oppressors. The clear teaching is that if the people wish to preserve their freedom, they have to do what is good before the eyes of God.

The second point, equally important, is that in spite of that clear parallelism between history as told by Israel and history as told by the surrounding nations, there are two very important differences. They both have to do with who this god is whose obedience is to be promoted in the telling of history.

The first such difference has to do with the moral nature of God, and therefore with the obedience that this god desires. The Babylonians believed that they were to serve the gods so that the gods in turn would bless the nation. The Phoenicians, Greeks, Romans, and all the other surrounding nations agreed on this point. Such service to the gods was mostly religious and consisted primarily of sacrifices and other acts of devotion by which the good will of the gods was earned. The ethical dimensions of service to the gods, though present, were minimal, and frequently contradictory, for the behavior that a god desired could very well be different from that which another god demanded. Thus, while Herodotus, for instance, tells the story of the Persian wars in order to promote civic virtue among his readers, the Greek gods do not live according to that virtue and do not demand it from their devotees. It is in Israel that service to God becomes first of all service to justice. This strange God of Israel, while still expecting sacrifices, offerings, and special celebrations, demands justice above all,

Your new moons and your appointed festivals
      my soul hates;
they have become a burden to me,
      I am weary of bearing them...

Wash yourselves; make yourselves clean;
      remove the evil of your doings
      from before my eyes;

cease to do evil,
        learn to do good;
seek justice,
        rescue the oppressed,
defend the orphan,
        plead for the widow.

Come now, let us argue it out, says the LORD.
(Isa. 1:14, 16–18a)

The second huge difference between the history of Israel and that of the surrounding nations has to do with the monotheistic faith of the Hebrews. If there is only one God, Creator and Lord of all that exists, history must necessarily be universal. If there is such a God, nothing can be left out of the sphere of history. This is the most notable contrast between history as the Hebrew Scriptures tell it and history as told by the surrounding nations. The *Nine Books of History* of Herodotus tell the story of the wars between the Greeks and Persians. While Herodotus speaks about the Egyptians, and even wrote an entire book on them, it is because Cambyses, King of Persia, conquered Egypt. If he writes about Assyria, it is for the same reason. When all has been said, the work of Herodotus is the story of Greece and its great enemy, Persia. (Although in all justice, one has to add that Herodotus shows himself to be more able than many historians, even today, to understand the values, perspectives, and lifestyle of the Persian enemy.) Thucydides wrote about the Peloponnesian wars. Cato's book deals with the *Origins*, certainly, but only Roman origins. Livy wrote a book *From the Foundation of Rome.* In contrast to all of this, Genesis begins with eleven chapters that make it very clear that the narrative that follows is the narrative of a particular people, and that even though that people has a special relationship with God, all peoples–that is, obviously, all those that Israel then knew– are part of a great "table of the nations." They are all part of God's creation.[1] If we then turn to Christian history, it is interesting to compare the genealogy in the gospel of Matthew with the one in Luke. Matthew begins with Abraham; Luke's chronology goes back to Adam. Luke the historian knows that the story that he is about to tell is grafted into the much wider history of the entire creation and all of humankind. That may be seen also in the manner in which he relates his own narrative to dates and events beyond the strict limits of his subject matter: "In the days of King Herod of Judea," "In those days a decree went out from Emperor Augustus...while Quirinius was governor of Syria." And later on: "In the fifteenth year of the reign of Emperor Tiberius, when Pontius Pilate was governor of Judea, and Herod was ruler of Galilee, and his brother Philip ruler of the region of Ituraea and Trachonitis, and Lysanias ruler of Abilene, during the high priesthood of Annas and Caiaphas," and so on, to the point that in the last chapters of the book of Acts such references appear constantly.

Luke does not do this in order to show off his erudition, nor simply in order to date the events that he tells. He does it, rather, in order to serve as a constant reminder that the history that he is narrating takes place within a wider context, that this entire context is part of God's creation, and that there, too, will God's purposes be fulfilled.

Biblical history deals specifically with a small sector of the human race. But it also reminds us from its very beginnings that the history of that small sector is part of a greater whole, that the story of Abraham is framed within the table of nations, that the story of Jesus has its roots in Abraham, that the story of the church takes place within the history of the Roman Empire.

This means that from a Christian point of view the phrase "universal history" is somewhat redundant. By definition, on the basis of Christian monotheism, history is universal. There is only one creation, one purpose, one history. Whatever histories we tell—be they the history of the church, of a nation, or of our own lives—are only a small portion of the Great History, the one that begins with creation and does not end until the final consummation.

The Particularity of Every History

On the other hand, while history is universal, no historian is. Every historian is particular, concrete, subject to the limits of the historian's circumstances, experiences, and questions. Whoever writes history from a Christian perspective is therefore faced by a difficult paradox: it is important to remember constantly that there is only one history, which includes all and everything, but it is also important to remember that what one tells is not only a small portion of that universal history but is even that portion as seen from a very particular and therefore limited perspective.

That is why history, even though it deals with the past, and the past cannot change, is always changing. History studies the past, but whoever studies history is in the present and reads the past from this present moment and from an expected future.[2] The result of all this is that a significant part of my task as a historian is to recover a past for my own present, and that for that reason many of the most important moments in history, and the conflicts that took place in them, were conflicts over the manner in which the past was to be interpreted and, above all, about who could claim it as an inheritance.

A Christian Reinterpretation of the History of Israel

In a way, that is the great conflict within the church in its first generation. The church is born in the midst of Israel and declares itself to be the heir to the traditions of Israel, and therefore to the promises made to Abraham. Christians claim that Jesus is the Christ, the anointed of God. They, and above all the Lord whom they follow, are the culmination of the history of Israel. But at the same time others who also claim to be heirs of the history of Israel read it in a very different way. Thus, we see in the New Testament repeated attempts to reinterpret that nation's history. The conflict between Jewish Christians and non-Christian Jews was a conflict over history.

This may be clearly seen in the episode in which the struggle over the possession of history results in the violence of the first Christian martyrdom. In Acts 7 Stephen is before the council and delivers a speech in which he summarizes the history of Israel. The story he tells is well known by his audience, and therefore most of his speech seems to be acceptable. But even so, Stephen is interpreting that history that is known to all in his own particular way, and that interpretation is the foundation for what he will eventually conclude. Thus, for instance, in this story of Moses, Stephen stresses the contrast between the way in which his own people received him at first and the plans that God had for him: "It was this Moses whom they rejected when they said, 'Who made you a ruler and a judge?' and whom God now sent as both ruler and liberator" (7:35). He then insists on this theme: "Our ancestors were unwilling to obey him; instead, they pushed him aside, and in their hearts they turned back to Egypt" (7:39).

Up to this point, his audience might be suspicious about the direction that the speech is taking. What Stephen is saying is indeed in the Bible. But Stephen's interpretation is not the one generally accepted.

This different interpretation reaches its high point when Stephen comes to the building of the temple. For the members of the council, the temple was the greatest manifestation of God's glory, as well as of the glory of Israel. But Stephen sees things differently. After speaking about the pilgrimage in the desert, and about how "our ancestors had the tent of testimony in the wilderness," Stephen interprets the building of the temple as an apostasy, or at least as a mistake: "But it was Solomon who built a house for him. Yet the Most High does not dwell in houses made with human hands" (7:47–48).

Then follows the harsher section, in verses 51–53, where Stephen establishes a parallelism between those ancient attitudes of the people and the attitudes of the present leaders of the council. By the time he comes to this point, we are not surprised that "when they heard these things, they became enraged and ground their teeth at Stephen" (7:54).

What is at stake here is precisely the question of who the true heirs of the history of Israel are, whether the heirs are the leaders of the council, who believe themselves to be the guardians of that history and its inheritance, or whether they are these newcomers who claim that Jesus is the Messiah, the anointed one, and that in him the promises made to Israel are being fulfilled.

What the church was doing in that first generation, as may be seen clearly in the New Testament, was not only claiming for itself the history of Israel but also reinterpreting that history from its own perspective in order to be able to claim it. In other words, the act itself of claiming history implies a new reading of that very history.

This could be illustrated by depicting history as a spiral in which each new turn, even while seemingly returning to themes that have been discussed before, does so from a new perspective, according to the circumstances of the moment. This is why history itself also has a history.

Thus, for instance, in the second century the church went back to the question of how it was to reclaim and to reinterpret the history of Israel. By then the problem was posed not only by those Jews who did not accept the Christian reinterpretation but also by some Christians who simply wished to do away with the entire history of Israel—or if not, at least to reinterpret it in such a way that it had no value for Christians. Such was the case of Marcion and his followers, as well as of several gnostic schools.

Marcion is not generally considered a historian. Actually his theology was such that he did not have much use for history. But in fact, at the very heart of Marcion's theology is his own interpretation of history. He saw creation as a serious mistake, the product of an inferior god, the Yahweh of the Old Testament, a god of law, of judgment, of punishment, and a god in marked contrast with the supreme God, the father of Jesus Christ, who is loving and forgiving, who has nothing to do with material creation nor with judgment and punishment, but only with the eternal salvation of all souls. This clearly implies that the history of Israel, as well as the entirety of human history, is simply part of that error that began with creation and will end with the destruction of all Yahweh's works.

This could be studied at several levels, but it may suffice to illustrate it by the manner in which Marcion interprets the beginnings of Christianity. According to him, among all the disciples of Jesus only Paul really understood Jesus' teachings. The others allowed themselves to be carried away by their Jewish traditions and understood what Jesus had to say in legalistic terms. This was not the case with Paul, who understood that the gospel is the message of the pure grace of God, a grace that simply forgives, a grace such that there is no word of judgment, a grace that is diametrically opposed to law. It was those first disciples led astray by their Jewish legalism who produced writings in which they made Jesus appear as the continuation of Yahweh's message. It was Judaizers of the same ilk who introduced in Paul's original epistles all those references to the Old Testament that now appear in them. Therefore, when Marcion proposed his canon of the New Testament—which included only the gospel of Paul's companion Luke and the epistles of Paul, all of it "cleansed" of "Judaizing" interpolations—what he was in fact doing was applying his own reading of history, and in particular of the history of the preceding century.

Among the gnostics, a similar example would be the sect of the "ophites," who derived this name from their claim that the hero in the story of Genesis is not God, but rather the serpent (in Greek, *ophis*). According to them, the serpent was the great liberator of humankind, for in offering the knowledge of good and evil it freed humankind from the ignorance to which the creator God had subjected it. It is not necessary to add that the ophites then read the entire history of the Old Testament in the opposite sense from the traditional Jewish and orthodox Christian readings. The same may be said about other similar groups, such as the Cainites, whose hero was Cain.

Clearly, this was a radical reinterpretation of the entire Old Testament tradition. In a way, what the Marcionites, the ophites, the Cainites, and so many other groups were doing was reinterpreting history and gleaning from it what best fit their own teachings or positions. Earlier, the very first generation of Jews who accepted Christianity had to reinterpret the history of Israel in order to claim that they were its faithful followers. Paul carried on a continuing struggle to have the Gentiles accepted as fellow heirs of the promises made to Abraham. Since eventually, at least among Christians, Paul's positions won the day, what was then debated in the second century was who Paul's true heirs and proper interpreters were, whether the Marcionites or the rest of the church. Therefore, what might have seemed to have been already solved during the first century reappeared in the second, though with a new face.

New Situations Lead to New Interpretations

The impact of a new situation is felt not only in the way in which previous questions are asked, as was the case with the interpretation of the Old Testament. New situations also bring about conflicts having to do with new questions, or perhaps with questions that appeared earlier only in embryonic form. If the first generations had to deal mostly with the conflict with traditional Judaism regarding the interpretation and inheritance of the Hebrew Scriptures, what came to the foreground by the second or the third generations was the organization of the church: who had the right to teach, who would make decisions, who would hold authority over others, and so forth. This was not a mere struggle for power. It was also the inevitable result of the felt need to preserve proper doctrine, to keep the unity of the church, to make certain that new and radical reinterpretations of history and doctrine, such as those of the Marcionites and the gnostics, did not take root in Christian congregations.

This led to a whole process of establishing rules and limits, deciding who had authority over what, and organizing ministries within the church following structures that became increasingly hierarchical.

One may see signs of this process in the New Testament itself, particularly in later books such as those that are often called "deuteropauline." There, especially in the pastoral epistles, there is an attempt to define the functions of bishops and deacons and especially to limit the place and authority of women in the church. Paul appears there as a very different person from the author of Romans, Galatians, or Philemon, and also different from the Paul whom Acts presents. In Philemon, Paul tells his friend to receive the runaway slave "as you would welcome me" (v. 17), and "no longer as a slave but more than a slave, a beloved brother...both in the flesh and in the Lord" (v. 16). In contrast, the Paul of the deuteropauline literature seems to be perfectly content with a situation in which a brother can own another. In Galatians, Paul says that in Christ there is neither male nor female (3:28), but in First Corinthians he says that when women preach they should cover their heads (1 Cor. 11:5).[3] In the later supposedly Pauline literature, they are simply told to remain silent.

These new developments and conflicts regarding the structure of the church and the place of women may be seen in the two main textual traditions through which the book of Acts has reached us. These are usually called the "Egyptian text" or "Common text," and the "Western text." Most scholars agree that in general the Common or Egyptian text is the original, and that the Western text is a revision, and sometimes an expansion of, that original. The Western text, produced precisely in the midst of those later efforts to regulate the life of the church and to limit the authority and the ministry of women, shows a clear anti-feminine prejudice. Let us see some examples.

According to the book of Acts, Priscilla and Aquila played an important role in Paul's ministry. In the Common text of Acts, they are always mentioned in that order, Priscilla and Aqulia, except once where the grammatical construction requires that Aquila be mentioned first. The Western text invariably inverts the order, speaking repeatedly of "Aquila and Priscilla." In Acts 17:12, the NRSV follows the Western text: "Many of them therefore believed, including not a few Greek women and men of high standing." But the Common text actually says that it was the women who were of high standing. At the end of the same chapter, where the Common text says "including Dionysius the Areopagite and a woman named Damaris, and others with them," the Western text simply says "including Dionysius the Areopagite and others."

What is happening here is that in the midst of an effort to regulate the life of the church, the earlier history of that very church is being reinterpreted. Both the deuteropauline epistles and the Western text of Acts were composed with that purpose, among others. As part of the same program, the deuteropauline epistles seek to limit the ministry of "widows," that is, of women who devoted all their time to the service of the church and the needy, and whom the church supported. These letters foster an attitude of suspicion in speaking of "widows who are really widows" (1 Tim. 5:3). Women who are younger than sixty years old and who have only been married once are not to be added to the official list of widows (1 Tim. 5:9), and they are generally encouraged to remarry and to devote themselves to family life rather than to the leadership and service of the church.

While we are heirs of the very first generation of Christians, we are also heirs of these later generations, which have taught us to read the story of the beginnings of the church as they did.

The book of Acts itself is an example of this sort of reading that we have been taught. The title, "Acts of the Apostles," is not part of the original, but was given to the book precisely at the time when the Western text was being produced. Upon reading that title, we immediately think that what we will find here is the story of how the apostles acted, and that therefore we will find also direct guidance for everything as we imitate the apostles.

However, if we carefully read the entire book, we immediately see that it is not really about the apostles. The eleven, and particularly Peter and John, seem to be the main actors at the beginning of the book. These eleven elect a twelfth, Matthias, of whom we hear no more. By the time we get to chapter 6 the twelve begin to wane. Even Peter disappears in chapter 12, reappears briefly in chapter 15, and then completely disappears, without a single word being said about what became of him.

Meanwhile, in chapter 6, seven other people appear. These seven are elected in order to manage the distribution of resources to the needy, particularly widows. We have become so accustomed to reading the book of Acts as if it were a manual of discipline for the church that we have come to call these seven people the "seven deacons," even though neither here nor anywhere else in the New Testament are they given such a title. (Their ministry is indeed called a *diakonia;* but the same word is equally applied to the ministry of the twelve.) Whatever the case may be, the twelve decide that they will be in charge of preaching and that these other seven will be managers. But in the very next verse we find Stephen, one of the seven, giving witness outside the church. By the next chapter we see Stephen, who according to the decision of the twelve is not supposed to be preaching, actually preaching the longest sermon in the entire book of Acts! Stephen is killed at the end of that chapter, but in the eighth chapter it is Philip, another of the seven, who is now preaching in Samaria, and then on the road to Gaza, to the Ethiopian eunuch. In chapter 9 Paul begins to take center stage, and on that basis one could imagine that the book is indeed about the apostles, since Paul himself will claim to be an apostle. But in fact the book is not about Paul either, for it simply ends without telling us what eventually became of Paul.

This shows that the book of Acts can be read in at least two ways. Most commonly, ever since the second century, people tend to read Acts as a sort of manual of discipline, or a guide for the government of the church. A different way, which is probably more akin to the situation in which the book was originally written, is to read Acts as a witness of the manner in which the Holy Spirit works and opens its own way, sometimes through the ministry and the decisions of the apostles and other church leaders, and sometimes in spite of those decisions, as is the case when Stephen and Philip preach. Thus, within the brief compass of two or three generations, the same events–and even a single document–can be read in more than one way. It is thus that the history of the church begins to develop its own history.

7

The Struggle over Greco-Roman History

Although the most urgent question for Christians of the first generation had to do with the history of Israel, soon other Christian generations–whose main context was no longer Israel, but the Greco-Roman world–had to face the question of the relationship between the gospel and the long and fruitful intellectual and political history of that Greco-Roman world.

Monotheism Requires a Single History

In the previous chapter I indicated that a monotheistic faith forces Christians to look at history as a whole. One of the main points of contrast between the various pagan religions and monotheism is that the former see the world and history as the stage where the various gods work out their conflicts, whereas the latter sees the world and history as a single whole. The polytheistic world is a multiverse rather than a universe. If Christianity is to be faithful to its vision of a single God, creator and sustainer of all that exists, that vision must be reflected in its own understanding of history–and not only of its own history, but of the entire history of God's creation.

Bluntly stated, this means that a church history whose concern is only the church and Christian believers, as if the rest of creation had nothing to do with the God of the church, is a pagan church history! (This certainly does not mean that there is not a place for church history as a distinct discipline. It does mean that such history must never forget that it is part of a single and grand history that embraces much more than the narrow limits of the church.)

The great intellectual leaders of Christianity in its early centuries understood this quite clearly. It is true that the great apologists of the second century–authors such as Justin Martyr and Athenagoras–wrote in order to show their pagan readers that Christian faith was not as absurd as often imagined. But it is also true, and less often said, that these apologists also wrote because the horizons of their faith forced them to do so. It was not only a matter of showing pagans that Christianity was reasonable. It was also a matter of seeing how, if it was true that Jesus Christ was the Lord and culmination of all history, that Lordship and that culmination related to the other human achievements of Greco-Roman philosophy and culture. If there is only one God, and if that God has come to us in Jesus Christ, somehow our faith must relate to everything else that God has been doing through the centuries, and still continues doing in various cultures and civilizations.

If Christianity is indeed the supreme revelation and action of the one and only God, then the gospel that the church proclaims must have something to do with everything both within and beyond the church. In the case of history, the gospel must somehow relate to every dimension and every corner of human history.

For the early church this was most urgently posed in three spheres: Hebrew tradition, Greco-Roman philosophy, and the civil order of society.

In the last chapter, we saw that the earliest historical concerns of Christians had to do with the first of these questions, the relationship between the gospel and Hebrew tradition. Since the manner in which these issues develop may be likened to a spiral, which at each turn returns to the same subject but under a different light and in different circumstances, the matter of the relationship between the church and Israel has repeatedly appeared. In the second century, Justin, Tatian, and others returned to it, as did Tertullian and Origen in the third, and Jerome, Ambrose, and others in the fourth. The process continued until we come in the twentieth century to Karl Barth and the Confessing Church in Nazi Germany. That particular episode is mentioned as a reminder that what is at stake in the various readings of history is not just history, but life itself. A polytheistic or pagan reading of history, even of church history, has dire consequences, not only for the church but also for the world.

The two other spheres in which the question was posed of the relationship between the gospel and the rest of human history were Greco-Roman culture and the civil order of society. The manner in which Christians responded to these questions has left an indelible mark on Christianity throughout its history, both for good and for evil.

The Gospel and Greco-Roman Culture

The manner in which most theologians responded to the first of these two questions—the relationship between the gospel and Greco-Roman culture—was first proposed by Justin Martyr in the second century. Much has been written about Justin and his doctrine of the logos, and it need not be repeated here. Briefly stated, Justin takes the philosophical doctrine of logos, of that reason that permeates all that exists and in virtue of which a human mind can comprehend reality, and then relates it with the prologue of the Fourth Gospel, which says that the logos of God became incarnate in Jesus Christ and that this logos is the light that shines on everyone who comes into this world. That being the case, Justin argues, any true knowledge that anyone has or has had is the result and the gift of that logos. Thus, Jesus Christ "is the logos of whom all humankind participates. Thus, those who in the past lived according to the logos, are in fact Christians, even though they were thought to be atheists, as was the case among the Greeks with Socrates and Herodotus."[1]

Thus, Justin's doctrine of the logos or the word of God becomes a means for Christians to appropriate any truth or any apparently valuable teaching that might have existed among the Greeks and Romans. But it is more than that. It is also a manner of reading the entire history of humankind so that in a sense it all becomes Christian history. In other words, the history of Greek philosophy is also part of the history of the activity of the same logos of God who has now been revealed to Christians.

This certainly does not mean that Justin is ready to affirm and accept every product of culture or philosophy. He knows about the errors of the philosophers, and even though he does not mock them as does Hermias in *The Mockery of Philosophers,* nor does he attack them as did his own disciple Tatian, he does know that the philosophers "frequently contradicted each other."[2] For Justin, the measure by which the doctrines of the philosophers are to be judged is the incarnation of Jesus Christ, and therefore he says that "our religion is higher than any human teaching, for the mere reason that the entire logos, who is Christ, and who has been revealed for us became body, and reason, and soul."[3]

Furthermore, the scope of what Justin proposes is such that he sees the gospel as the culmination not only of Judaism—which others before him had already done—and of Greek philosophy, but of all human culture and even of creation itself. Regarding culture, Justin points out that the cross is at the very foundation of every human activity, for "one does not sail on the sea without this sign of victory"—the mast and yard—and "without it the land is not plowed, nor do diggers or artisans do their work without instruments shaped like it." As to creation itself, Justin claims that the human being has been made in the form of a cross.[4]

All this sounds somewhat childish, and may be so. But it also involves a vast cosmic vision of the action and purposes of God. The gospel and its cross are not a last-minute solution, a response to the crisis of sin, as they have become for many Christians. The gospel and the cross are part of the very structure of the universe. Everything points to them, so that even cultural advances among the pagans unwittingly bear the sign of the gospel.

Behind all this stands a vision of Christian history that does not begin with the preaching of the gospel, nor even with the birth of Jesus, but has its roots before the foundation of the world, in the eternal designs of God. Even though Justin's examples may seem childish, there is one point on which Christians do well heeding him: the history that is of concern for Christians goes back to the very beginnings of God's creative work.

It was this view of history that allowed Christians to enter the arena of philosophical dialogue and to see the positive elements of the culture around them. Without such a vision, or one like it,

Christianity would have become a sect, a matter of a corner, a separate segment in a world that was already segmented among various powers like a pagan world divided among its various deities.

Beginning with Justin, there is an entire tradition within the Christian church—a tradition that soon became the majority of believers—that claims a history in which Christianity is not only the culmination of the promises made to Israel but also the crown of Greek philosophy. As Justin, Clement, Origen, and many others would say, Christianity is "the true philosophy."

The classical expression of this vision of history is to be found late in the second century in Clement of Alexandria, who claims that God gave the prophets to the Jews and the philosophers to the Greeks as two similar covenants announcing the new covenant in Jesus Christ—or, using a simile Clement himself uses, as two oarsmen moving the same boat.

Once again, this implies not only a vision of Christianity and philosophy as complementary to each other, about which much has been written, but also a vision of history as a single reality, like a ship that God moves by means of different oarsmen, but all leading to the same goal in Christ.

In a word, if with Paul and the other writers of the New Testament, Christianity claimed for itself the Hebrew tradition as part of its own history, then with Justin, Clement, and their many contemporaries Christianity claimed for itself the Greek philosophical tradition, making it part of a single and undivided history.

Three Dangers

Such a doctrine of the logos certainly has its dangers, and at least three of these are worthy of note.

The first danger has been discussed so often and thoroughly that a brief mention should suffice. In brief, the danger is that in the inevitable dialogue between philosophy and Christian doctrine the former be given too much authority. Thus, much of Christian tradition soon began interpreting the reign or kingdom of God in terms of the world of ideas of Plato; the God and Father of our Lord Jesus Christ became the first unmoved mover; and the resurrection of the body gave way to the immortality of the soul. The apologetic bridge bears traffic in both directions.

The second danger is in reducing the presence of the logos or word of God, of that light that shines on everyone who comes to this world, to the purely intellectual–that Christianity may be seen only, as the ancients would say, as "the true philosophy," and lose other equally important dimensions. Thus, for instance, the principle of the universal presence of the logos has been used to explain why a particular people already exhibited monotheistic tendencies, why they believed in life after death, and so on. If a nation already had a certain conception of God before the preaching of the gospel arrived, it was said this was due to the presence of the logos or word of God in that nation. But the same principle has not been applied equally to other matters. For instance, if there is in a nation or a people a strong sense of the justice that must reign in human relationships; if there is a sense of solidarity; if there is compassion toward the weak, the elderly, and the unprotected; if there is a government that somehow tries to produce and sustain a social order, all that has little or nothing to do with the logos. In other words, the doctrine of the logos, thus employed, has contributed greatly to what could be called the "doctrinalization" of Christianity, as if all that God wishes and requires of us were simply a series of doctrines and beliefs–or, in other words, that we subscribe to "the true philosophy." (At this point it is important to point out, however, that for Justin and his contemporaries "philosophy" was not only a matter of doctrines and beliefs but also of a style of life. People would speak, for instance, of the "philosophical life" as one devoted to certain principles of justice, wisdom, simplicity, and so forth. It was only much later that "philosophy" became mostly limited to matters of doctrines and that Christianity tended to be "doctrinalized" as the "true philosophy.")

The third danger is even more insidious. This is the danger that the doctrine of the logos be employed only in those cases in which it becomes necessary, forgetting that there must also be a presence of the logos in those peoples whom Christians can conquer and convince by other means. Throughout history, Christian evangelists and missionaries have tended to find the logos only in those cultures and peoples they could not conquer or subdue, and to forget the logos in their encounters with supposedly "inferior" cultures and people. In the latter case it was not a matter of finding out what those cultures had to contribute to Christianity and its own self-understanding. Here it was rather a matter of how to communicate to a heathen culture the faith given once and for all—not just to the apostles and prophets, but also to their North Atlantic heirs. That is why such encounters were marginalized, usually pushed out of the field of church history and into the separate field of the history of missions or the history of the expansion of Christianity. Church history studied how Justin Martyr interpreted Christianity in dialogue with Greco-Roman culture, but the issue of polygamy in some African cultures and how African Christians struggled with it are part of the history of missions. Church history studies the significance of the printing press for the early stages of the Protestant Reformation, but the significance of the horse for the conquest and colonization of the Western Hemisphere has nothing to do with church history. Indeed, if African Christians or Native American Christians somehow allowed their traditions to color their understanding and their practice of the faith, the specter of syncretism immediately arose, thus implying not only that their Christianity was not really part of the history of the church but even that it was not part of the church at all. Needless to say, this has done much damage to such supposedly inferior cultures and peoples, as well as to the church itself, which has found it difficult to be deeply rooted in those cultures.

At any rate, if the first great episode in Christian historiography was the claiming of the Hebrew tradition in the first century, the second great episode was the claiming of the philosophical tradition of the Greco-Roman world, beginning in the second century.

The Gospel and Civil Government

There was still another sphere of human history that had not been incorporated into Christian historiography. This was the sphere of civil government, of political history. Certainly, as I have already pointed out, from as early as the time when the gospel of Luke was written some Christians felt the need to place the Christian narrative within the context of the political order and their own chronology and genealogies within the context of the chronologies and genealogies of emperors, governors, patriarchs, and so on. From a very early date the church was forced to take into account the state within which it existed. This can be seen in the gospels, but becomes crystal clear in the last chapters of the book of Acts. Very soon after that, as persecution increased, the matter of the relationship between the Christian church and the civil government became one of life and death. But it was not until the fourth century that a Christian historiography finally evolved that included the political order, not only as a context but also as part of the content of Christian history. It was in that fourth century, particularly through the work and the interest of Eusebius of Caesarea (c.260–c.340), usually called "the father of church history," that the direction was set for much of Christian historiography–some of it lasting until our days.

History, Apology, and Philosophy in the Work of Eusebius

As a historian, Eusebius has been heavily criticized and even mistreated by later generations. There is ample reason to criticize his historical method. However, before attempting such criticism it is important to place him in his context and to see the scope of his work. Sometime before writing his famous *Church History,* Eusebius wrote the *Chronicles of the Hellenes and the Barbarians,* which was actually an adaptation of a similar work by Julius Africanus (c.160–c.240). What is remarkable in these chronicles is that they deal with the Chaldeans, the Assyrians, the Hebrews, the Egyptians, the Greeks, and the Romans, presenting a comparative chronology in parallel columns. Thus, it is what today we would call a "world history"–"world," obviously within the parameters of the times. That chronology begins with Abraham, for Eusebius, with more critical sense than many of his contemporaries and even more than Archbishop Usher, felt that the narratives before Abraham should not be taken literally. At any rate, Eusebius has an apologetic purpose, and his *Chronicles,* in spite of all their erudition, are simply a new variation of the ancient argument employed both by Jews and by Christians that Moses was before Plato, and that therefore any common points or views they share are due to Plato's having learned them from Moses and from the Hebrew tradition.

Like the *Chronicles,* much of the work of Eusebius is apologetic. His two parallel writings, the *Praeparatio Evangelica* and the *Demostratio Evangelica,* seem to be an attempt to refute the fifteen books *Against the Christians* by the Neoplatonist scholar Porphyry. In the *Praeparatio,* Eusebius affirms the superiority of Judaism over paganism and claims that Judaism was given as a preparation for the gospel. In the *Demostratio,* he asserts that the law of Moses was given in order to serve as a bridge between the religion of the patriarchs, which was universal, and Christianity, which is called also to be universal. From there he moves on to explain and try to offer proof for the main Christian doctrines.

It is important to remember this, because Eusebius is an apologist at heart, and his famous *Church History* is also an apology. While it is true that Eusebius manifests a much more refined critical ability than most historians of his time, and offers ample documentation by quoting his sources, and while it is also true that he is willing to do this even though the fluidity and the style of his writing may suffer, still his purpose is to show the truth of Christianity.

Furthermore, in a certain sense Eusebius did not really believe that a history of the church could be written, for he was so influenced by the Platonic tradition that he had inherited from Origen that he could not really conceive of the church and especially of its doctrine as part of the historical process. A German historian of the nineteenth century has said that for Eusebius "the church is not a historical fact, but is suprahistorical, transcendent, and strictly eschatological from its very beginning, without any possibility of historical mutation."[5] Or as Yale professor Jaroslav Pelikan has declared, Eusebius was "a historian who did not believe in history."[6] For Eusebius, any true change in the life of the church would be a sign of weakness or untruth, for truth itself must be immutable and transcendent. He is not actually writing about the development of the church—how it was shaped, adapted, and so forth—but is rather compiling a series of data about the life of the church, which he has organized chronologically, data such as lists of bishops, important events, persecutions, martyrdoms, significant authors, and so on.

These data Eusebius compiled with a purpose that, at least in the final form of his book, was apologetic. Most scholars agree that out of the ten books of the *Church History* of Eusebius, the first seven were written before the persecution of Diocletian, that is, before the year 303. Had Eusebius completed his work at that point, we would have seen that his purposes in writing were (1) to strengthen and encourage Christians facing persecution by telling the story of exemplary martyrs; (2) to compile data about the various heresies and to warn his readers against them; (3) as part of the recitation of heresies, to collect lists of bishops in the main churches, thus establishing a connection between the present bishops and the apostles; and (4) to conserve important texts and facts by quoting authors whose works Eusebius had at hand in the Christian library of Cesarea, but to which his readers would have no access.

The Changing Context of Eusebius

However, after the great persecution of Diocletian and the sudden end of persecution with the so-called "Edict of Milan," in which Emperors Licinius and Constantine put an end to persecution, Eusebius wrote three more books, in which he told the horrors of the great persecution and praised both Constantine and Licinius for having brought peace to the church. Since shortly thereafter there was a falling out between Licinius and Constantine, who eventually became sole master of the Empire by defeating Licinius, Eusebius produced a final version of his work, in which he deleted his previous praise of Licinius, and added even more favorable words about Constantine. Apparently he also edited the seven books that he had written earlier so as to make the whole story flow toward its high point after the conversion of Constantine.

In its final version the *Church History* of Eusebius has the clear purpose of showing that the new order under the direction of Constantine was the result of the eternal designs of God, who had given to humankind not only the Hebrew tradition and Greek philosophy but also the Roman Empire, all of them as preparation for Christianity. Thus, while the very first Christians claimed for themselves the Hebrew tradition, and those of the second century began claiming the philosophical tradition, now Eusebius in the fourth was ready to claim for himself and for Christianity the entire political history of Rome. Just as the biblical tradition was destined to be joined with the philosophical, so also was the Roman state destined to be united to the church. In this context, Eusebius approvingly quotes the words of second-century Bishop Melito of Sardis:

> And a most convincing proof that our doctrine flourished for the good of an empire happily begun, is this–that there has no evil happened since Augustus' reign, but that, on

the contrary, all things have been splendid and glorious, in accordance with the prayers of all. Nero and Domitian, alone, persuaded by certain calumniators, have wished to slander our doctrine, and from them it has come to pass that the falsehood has been handed down, in consequence of an unreasonable practice which prevails of bringing slanderous accusations against the Christians.[7]

In other words, divine providence was the reason why the Roman Empire was born together with Christianity, so that they could support and benefit each other. Melito lived in the second century, which in some ways was the golden age of the Roman Empire, before a series of debacles took place, and therefore he could affirm that nothing really evil had taken place since the times of Caesar Augustus and Jesus, that only Nero and Domitian had persecuted Christians, and that they had done this because they were misinformed. (Even though Melito's writing was addressed to Emperor Marcus Aurelius, who also persecuted Christians, and therefore Melito seems to be implying that this emperor also is ill informed.)

Persecution Becomes a Misunderstanding

Now, after so many years of persecution, Eusebius has a problem. He wishes to claim that the Roman Empire is part of a providential preparation for the gospel and to affirm that the recent accommodation between that empire and the church is the culmination of the very purpose for which the former was created. But the truth is that for several generations the Roman Empire has persecuted Christians. Therefore, Eusebius is forced to claim that none of the earlier emperors had good reason to persecute Christians. Maximin did so because he was jealous of his predecessor, who had been a friend of Christians; Decius, for similar reasons; Valerian, because he was deceived by the chief of the Magi in Egypt; Aurelian, because his advisers misled him; and so on. In a word, the persecutions were simply a great mistake on the part of the Roman Empire, which should have always looked upon the church as its natural ally. Those who persecuted Christians were insane, jealous, or ill informed.

It was this interpretation of persecution that Eusebius bequeathed to later Christian generations. It is true that during the period itself of persecution Christians insisted that they were wrongly persecuted, since they prayed for the Roman Empire and its authorities and led a specific style of life that did not harm anyone. This is repeatedly affirmed in ancient texts. But this is not quite the same as claiming that the persecutions were simply a great mistake on the part of Roman authorities.

Had the persecutions been due only to a misunderstanding by imperial authorities, one would expect that as the Romans learned more about the church and its faith, persecution would abate. But what happened was exactly the opposite. Persecutions, rather than waning, became increasingly harsh. Not only that, but they also became more widespread and sophisticated, ordering for instance, that Christians turn over their copies of scripture; attacking the leaders rather than the rank and file; and, toward the end, seeking to produce apostates rather than martyrs.

Furthermore, in spite of commonly held beliefs, the truth is that those who ordered the persecution of Christians were not always the worst emperors. On the contrary, some of the staunchest persecutors of Christians were also among the best emperors—those who rebuilt the state, who organized its defense, who restored and developed the economy, and so on.

However, Eusebius wrote his *Church History* within his own particular scheme of things, and that scheme forced him to depict persecution as a grave error on the part of Roman authorities. According to that scheme, God had been preparing humankind for the advent of Christianity since the remotest times. In the first chapters of his great work, Eusebius speaks about the patriarchs and the Hebrew tradition as a preparation for the gospel. Although he does not argue explicitly for that position in his history, Eusebius certainly belongs to the Platonic tradition of Justin, Clement of Alexandria, and Origen, who held that God had also given the philosophical tradition as a preparation for the advent of Christ. Eusebius was further convinced that God likewise prepared the Roman Empire as the context for that advent, and that therefore the best of the Roman tradition belonged to Christians, just as Justin had declared earlier that the best of pagan philosophy belonged to Christians. Eusebius embedded this notion, which already appeared in embryonic fashion in Melito, in his great history of the church and thus transmitted it to later generations, to the point that to this day it is common to begin telling the story of the church by affirming that the *pax romana,* the Roman roads, and an entire series of circumstances were providential preparations for the expansion of the gospel.

Within the scheme of Eusebius, Constantine's conversion is the culmination of God's plan both for the church and for the Roman Empire. That is why Eusebius can end his *Church History* with words that seem to imply that with Constantine and his actions the reign of God has arrived:

> All fear therefore of those who had formerly afflicted them was taken away from men, and they celebrated splendid and festive days. Everything was filled with light, and those who before were downcast beheld each other with beaming eyes. With dances and hymns, in city and country, they glorified first of all God the universal King, because they had been thus taught, and then the pious emperor with God-beloved children. There was oblivion of past evils and forgetfulness of every deed of impiety; there was enjoyment of present benefits and expectation of those yet to come. Edicts full of clemency and laws containing tokens of benevolence and true piety were issued in every place by the victorious emperor. Thus after all tyranny had been purged away, the empire which belonged to them was preserved firm and without a rival for Constantine and his sons alone. And having obliterated the godlessness of their predecessors, recognizing the benefits conferred upon them by God, they exhibited their love of virtue and their love of God, and their piety and gratitude to the Deity, by the deeds which they performed in the sight of all men.[8]

Elsewhere, in a speech celebrating the thirtieth anniversary of Constantine's accession to the imperial throne, Eusebius says of Constantine that "invested as he is with a semblance of heavenly sovereignty, he directs his gaze above, and frames his earthly government according to the pattern of that divine original, feeling strength in his conformity to the monarchy of God."[9]

The Consequences of Eusebius

Some might consider Eusebius a sycophant—and to a measure this may even be justified. But that is not the most serious consequence of his work. The most serious is that throughout this process Eusebius was offering a reading of Christian history that could lead—and indeed in many cases has led—to dire consequences.

The first characteristic of such a reading is that it is ecclesiocentric. The designs of God are always measured in terms of the church. Thus, for instance, those emperors who persecuted the church were evil, and Constantine was good because he defended it. At the beginning of his *Life of Constantine,* Eusebius literally affirms that he will only mention the religious aspects of that life. Eusebius had to limit his consideration of the life of Constantine to religious matters because even though Constantine restored the unity of the Empire and revitalized its economic life, he also committed all sorts of injustice and abuse, which Eusebius did not wish to mention. Furthermore, practically all the actions of Constantine that Eusebius praised were those that produced direct benefit to the church. The main exception is a short paragraph in which he praises the emperor's liberality toward orphans and the poor.

Significantly, throughout his *Life of Constantine,* as well as in *Church History,* Eusebius implies that the culmination of history is the church itself and the support it enjoys from the Empire. Little is said about Jesus Christ as the culmination of history, or of his presence in the general history of humankind. In a word, sacred history has become completely detached from secular history. This is particularly sad since in his own *Chronicles* Eusebius shows that he knew the general history of the various neighboring peoples and nations.

Such ecclesiocentric evaluation of events, governments, and policies has lasted for a long time. At about the same time as Eusebius, Lactantius wrote his treatise *On the Death of the Persecutors,* with the thesis that all those who persecuted the church were terrible rulers and suffered almost indescribably painful and shameful deaths. Apparently, all that matters to Lactantius as he evaluates a government is its attitude toward the church. In my own continent of Latin America, and among Protestants, we have even come to the point of defending and blessing a dictator for the sole reason that he claims to be one of us. Therefore, let us not be too hasty in condemning Eusebius, but let us rather confess how tempting the ecclesiocentric lure is.

Second, as I have already mentioned, because of his Platonic tendencies Eusebius understood the church as a celestial, immutable reality, much like the eternal ideas of Plato. This means that history never really touches the heart of the church. The church does not evolve. The church does not change. Above all, the church does not err, not because its members do not err, but rather because the true church is an immutable reality. That is why one could say that Eusebius was not really writing a history of the church. His work said nothing about the high and the low points, the straight and twisted ways of the church, but limited itself to events, placing all of them under the perspective of the church. Since by then Christianity had become quite "doctrinalized," and since because of his Platonic perspective Eusebius believed that all that changed was false, all that could he do was to present the church as an immutable reality whose accidents may change, but whose substance remains.

This understanding of the church as a suprahistorical, immutable, and spiritual reality would eventually lead to the day when the church would consider itself capable of judging the state and all of society, but would not be willing to have itself be judged. The process was long, and reached its high point in the year 1300, in the bull of Boniface VIII, *Unam Sanctam*:

> Therefore both swords, the spiritual as well as the material, are in the power of the church. But the latter is to be exercised on the Church's behalf and the former by the Church; the former in the hand of the priest, the latter in that of kings and soldiers, but at the beck and sufferance of the priest.
>
> One sword, however, must be beneath the other, and temporal authority must be subjected to spiritual.
>
> Therefore, if the temporal power errs it shall be judged by the power spiritual; if the lesser spiritual power errs, its judge is its superior; but if the highest spiritual power errs, it can be judged by God alone and not by man.[10]

A third and final characteristic of this sort of historical interpretation also has many serious consequences for the life of the church. Eusebius' reading of church history was not only ecclesiocentric and suprahistorical; it had also lost much of the countercultural and even subversive nature of early Christianity. The reason why the empire persecuted Christians was not a mistake, nor the madness of some emperors, nor the jealousy of others. The real reason the Empire persecuted Christians was that it saw in the Christian faith much that was incompatible with the values and interests of the Empire. In the second century, Celsus, a pagan and cultured enemy of Christianity, correctly pointed out that were all Romans to become Christians and refuse to join the army, the Empire would be left defenseless before the neighboring barbarians. Celsus also complained that among Christians even the most ignorant were considered as worthy teachers, that is, that social distinctions were obliterated. Already toward the end of the first century, while Domitian claimed to be lord of all, Christians insisted that the Lord was Jesus Christ and that there was no one above him. A few years later, early in the second century, Trajan was concerned because Christians in Bithynia refused to burn incense before his image, to which those Christians would probably have replied, as eighteen centuries later other Christians replied in Nazi Germany, "we repudiate the false teaching that there are areas of our life in which we belong not to Jesus Christ, but to another lord."[11] Imperial propaganda proclaimed the blessings of the *pax romana,* and over against it Christians spoke of a coming reign of peace and justice. The mere proclamation of the reign of God is itself a critique of all the reigns of this world. It was for these things that James, Peter, and Paul gave their life. It was for this that Polycarp was burned, and Perpetua and Felicitas were thrown to the beasts. And now Eusebius tells us that it was all a sad mistake!

Perhaps the mistake is both Eusebius' and ours, accustomed as we are to reading the history of the ancient church through the eyes of Eusebius and invested as we are in adapting to the values around us. No matter what the case may be, there is no doubt that history not only has a history, but also serious consequences!

8

The Struggle over Secular History

As was to be expected, the work of Eusebius was continued by historians of other generations, who sought to bring it up to date. However, the Empire about which Eusebius wrote would soon face serious crises, and these in turn would require new readings of history. Therefore, though much of church history written immediately after Eusebius was a mere continuation or appendix to his work, there soon were historians who had to face the new reality of a political system that was no longer run by Romans, but by Franks, Goths, Lombards, and others. After a brief word about the immediate followers of Eusebius, I shall turn to those who, under new circumstances, produced new interpretations of history, and particularly of the relationship between the history of nations and the history of the church.

The Continuation of Eusebius' Work

Just as more recent histories of the church that have become classic have required repeated updates, the work of Eusebius also required such updating. In the West, Rufinus of Aquileia translated it into Latin around the year 400, but he also brought it up to date to 395. In the East, Arian scholar Sabinus of Heracleia wrote a *History of the Councils,* which told the story of the Arian controversy up to the year 365, but which has been lost. Also lost is almost the entirety of the twelve books on *Church History* by Philostorgius.

In the fifth century three different authors, working independently of one another and all writing in Greek, composed church histories that are practically appendices to the history of Eusebius, and that cover the period from the time of Constantine to the first third of the fifth century.

Socrates, called "the historian" or "the scholastic" in order to distinguish him from the famous philosopher of the same name, wrote a *Church History* that is clearly intended to be an appendix to Eusebius, for it begins a few years before the ending of the work of Eusebius—with the abdication of Diocletian in 305—and continues to 450, on the eve of the Council of Chalcedon. Socrates declares himself to be a continuator of the work of Eusebius, while also improving on his predecessor's discussion of Arianism. He begins his work by declaring that

> Eusebius, surnamed Pamphilus, writing the History of the Church in ten books, closed it with that period of the emperor Constantine, when the persecution which Diocletian had begun against the Christians came to an end. Also in writing the life of Constantine, this same author has but slightly treated of matters regarding Arius, being more intent on the rhetorical finish of his composition and the praises of the emperor, than on an accurate statement of facts. Now, as we propose to write the details of what has taken place in the churches since his time to our own day, we begin with the narration of the particulars which he has left out.[1]

Apparently, Socrates made use of the materials that had been compiled by Sabinus of Heracleia, but reinterpreted them in defense of the Nicene faith.

The second of the three people who continued the work of Eusebius was Sozomen (c.400–c.450). His purpose was to retell the same story, but to bring back into it the rhetorical elegance of the ancient Greeks, which Eusebius as well as Socrates had sacrificed in favor of greater documentation.

The third of these Greek successors of Eusebius was Theodoret of Cyrus, who wrote his five books on *Church History* about the year 450, while he was exiled in Apamea. Theodoret belonged to the christological school of Antioch, which had fallen into disrepute when the Council of Ephesus in 431 condemned Nestorius, patriarch of Constantinople. Jointly with Theodoret, other leaders of the same theological school were accused of heresy. Therefore, the history that Theodoret wrote, and which goes up to 428, sought among other things to defend Antiochean theologians such as Diodore of Tarsus and Theodore of Mopsuestia, while criticizing the opposing school of Alexandria. Like Socrates, Theodoret declares himself to be a follower and continuator of the work of Eusebius:

> Eusebius of Palestine has written a history of the Church from the time of the holy Apostles to the reign of Constantine, the prince beloved of God. I shall begin my history from the period at which his terminates.[2]

In the next century, that is, the sixth, Evagrius the Scholastic also wrote another history that was based on those by Socrates, Sozomen, and Theodoret, and included the period between 431 and 594. This is one of our main sources for the details of the christological controversies that shook the East after the condemnation of Nestorius.

At about the same time, Cassiodorus (c.487–c.580) led and participated in the project of translating and coordinating the histories of Eusebius and his continuators Socrates, Sozomen, and Theodoret into a single history in twelve books in Latin. This *Tripartite History* became the most widely used text on church history throughout the Middle Ages. Since it is merely a compilation and summary of the works of Eusebius and his three main Greek successors, the *Tripartite History* is written from a perspective similar to that of Eusebius' *Church History,* and therefore this perspective dominated the medieval study of the history of the church.

The Inclusion of the Germanic Peoples

Between the fourth century, when Eusebius wrote his *Church History,* and the sixth, when Cassiodorus wrote his *Tripartite History,* some very important events took place. These events are commonly called "the barbarian invasions." For a long time, a number of Germanic peoples had threatened the borders of the Empire. But toward the end of the fourth century, and especially beginning in the fifth, in a successive series of migratory waves, these nations broke through the barriers of the Empire, crossed its borders, and settled in it. Most of them were not even mentioned in ancient chronicles or histories, be they Roman or Christian. When the Germanic peoples were mentioned, it usually was in passing, or they were seen as an enemy whom the Romans should resist or at best civilize.

Now the descendants of those invaders, having been converted to Christianity and to a certain point Romanized, began writing history. How were they to do so? They were not part of that history that according to Eusebius had culminated in Constantine. If only "sacred history" is important, what value should be ascribed to the history of these Germanic peoples before their conversion to Christianity? Cassiodorus, who produced the *Tripartite History,* was a functionary of the Gothic king Teodoric and wrote also a *History of the Goths,* which has unfortunately been lost, but the purpose of which seems to have been to show the glories of the Goths even before they settled in Roman territory.

Besides Cassiodorus, four important writers sought to include their own Germanic ancestry within the history of the church.

The first of these was Jordanes, a Goth who in the middle of the sixth century wrote a *History of the Goths,* which he may well have taken mostly from the lost work of Cassiodorus. Jordanes tried to cover the entire history of the Goths, beginning with their remote origins in Scandinavia and leading to the disappearance of Ostrogothic power in Italy, since by the time Jordanes was writing, in the middle of the sixth century, the Ostrogothic kingdom in Italy had already disappeared. Although a Goth in origin, Jordanes was a Romanized monk. Therefore, while he sympathized with the Goths, he was particularly interested in the Romans, and was even convinced that the Roman Empire, which by then was in fact the Byzantine Empire, had been called by God to continue indefinitely and to become a universal empire.

The second of these "barbarian" historians is Gregory of Tours (538–594), whom some consider the father of the history of France. Gregory was a native of Alvernia, in what today is France. His grandfather, also called Gregory, was famous for his devotion and holiness. Gregory himself was an admirer of Saint Martin of Tours, who lived two centuries before him and to whom Gregory attributed his miraculous recovery from an illness. Among Gregory's many works is *History of the Franks,* in ten books. In the second book, Gregory reaches the baptism of Clovis, and therefore, he speaks of the Franks mostly as Christians. The last six books are for the most part a chronicle of events during Gregory's lifetime. Therefore, what is of particular interest to us here is the first book, where Gregory speaks of the origins of the Franks. He claims that they descended from the Trojans, who were in turn descendants of Japheth, son of Noah. While this is clearly no more than a folk tale, it is interesting to note that Gregory tries to root the Franks both in the classical tradition of Troy and in the biblical tradition of Noah and Japheth. While Justin and Clement would declare themselves heirs of Hebrew Scripture and of Greek philosophy, and while Eusebius would declare himself at once a Roman and a Christian, now Gregory would claim a similar dual rootage for himself and his ancestors.

The third "barbarian" historian to be considered here is Venerable Bede (673–735), author of the *Church History of the English People,* who lived a century and a half after Gregory of Tours. In spite of its title, Bede's history does not deal only with the church and religious matters, but is an entire history of England from the time of Julius Caesar to the year 731. He is mostly interested in religious and ecclesiastical subjects, but even so he also tells the political history of the land, with its successive invasions, inner conflicts, and so on.

The last of these four historians is Paul Warnefrid, generally known as Paul the Deacon, who died in Monte Cassino in 799, leaving his *History of the Lombards* incomplete. Like the other three, Paul is interested in the origins of his people even before their first contacts with Christianity.

In summary, as historian Beryl Smalley says,

> Another urgent problem faced barbarian historians. Their
> models tended to separate sacred from secular history:
> could the history of a barbarian people follow such a
> division or must the two kinds of history be amalgamated?
> Barbarian history forbad the separation of its subject-
> matter into two parts. Conversion to Christianity, whether
> Catholicism or Arianism was chosen, marked a turning-
> point in a people's history. It affected their way of life,
> their institutions and their relations with their neighbours.
> Jordanes, Gregory of Tours and Paul the Deacon include
> religious history as an integral part of their stories. Bede
> made an attempt at separation; he concentrated on the
> Church, and he called his book *The Ecclesiastical History of
> the English People.* Secular history comes into it however.
> There is a larger element of the secular in Bede's *History*
> than there is in Eusebius'. The fortunes and preferences
> of English kings bore heavily on the endowment of
> churches and monasteries and on the careers of
> churchmen. The mixture of sacred and secular in
> historiography had come to stay.[3]

It would be possible and illuminating to establish a parallelism
between the situation of those Goths, Lombards, and Franks who
set out to write their own histories and the situation of present-
day Latin American church historians. We are Christian, and as
such we are grafted into the history of Abraham and his
descendants, as well as into the history of the church. But
Christianity did not reach our shores until 1492. Does this mean
that as Christians we ought to begin our history on that date? Or
is there a different way of reading and writing history? If our
perspective is ecclesiocentric, like that of Eusebius, and if, as we
have often been taught in theological circles—Protestant as well as
Catholic—the only really important history is our church history,
our history as Christians, what has traditionally been called "sacred
history," and we then somehow wish to claim the rest of our history,
we are free to do so, but always remembering that what we are
writing is "secular history." This is an untenable position.
Therefore, it is not mere coincidence that in Latin America there

has been serious questioning of the classical, easy, but very dangerous distinction between a "sacred history" and a "secular history." In this, we are similar to those early "barbarian" historians.

The Stages of History

Let us return to antiquity. Besides the historians whom we have been discussing, there were other authors and thinkers who were not historians but were very much interested in history and its interpretation. This is not surprising since, once again, Christian monotheism requires that one look at reality as a whole. In the field of history, from a very early date this led Christian thinkers to seek to look at history as a whole. This has always been particularly important for Christians, who have always held that the doctrine of creation and the hope for a final consummation require that history have a beginning and an end.

From a very early time, there was speculation about the duration of history and its various stages. This was usually done on the basis of scripture, and particularly with reference to the six days of creation. One of the first to develop such a scheme was Sextus Julius Africanus, who in the third century wrote the *Chronologies* (also known as *Chronicle*). He attempted to develop a worldwide chronology on the basis of what he took to be the biblical chronology. According to Julius Africanus, the world was created fifty-five hundred years before Christ, that is, five and a half "days" of a thousand years each, and at the end of the sixth day the great and final sabbath will begin, which is the millennium. The work of Julius Africanus was lost, but part of it seems to have survived in the *Chronicle* of Eusebius of Caesarea, who did employ it, but left aside its millennialist eschatology and its expectation of a relatively imminent return of Jesus. Lactantius, early in the fourth century, adopted a similar scheme, which led him to think that human history would last at most two hundred years beyond his own time. Since the work of Julius Africanus has been lost, Lactantius is a good exponent of this sort of speculation, which probably will bring to mind similar speculations circulating even today:

> Therefore, since all the works of God were completed in
> six days, the world must continue in its present state

through six ages, that is, six thousand years. For the great day of God is limited by a circle of a thousand years, as the prophet shows, who says, "In Thy sight, O Lord, a thousand years are as one day." And as God laboured during those six days in creating such great works, so His religion and truth must labour during these six thousand years, while wickedness prevails and bears rule. And again, since God, having finished His works, rested the seventh day and blessed it, at the end of the six thousandth year all wickedness must be abolished from the earth, and righteousness reign for a thousand years; and there must be tranquility and rest from the labours which the world now has long endured.[4]

Thus, the theme of a history that begins and ends within a certain time is common in Christian antiquity. And so is the notion that after the pattern of the six days of creation, history itself will last six thousand years.

Even within this context, there remained the question of which paradigm Christians would use to interpret that process leading from beginning to end. Here there were at least three significantly different possibilities. First, the paradigm of progress, which is perhaps the most common today. According to this paradigm, history is a process that in spite of its many turns and its ups and downs, moves toward a final consummation that will be better than the beginning. The most common paradigm in antiquity was exactly the opposite. The "golden age" was in the past, and the historical process was one of decadence and disintegration. A third option was the cyclical paradigm. History repeats itself, and everything turns back to an earlier situation. Thus, the first paradigm may be called the paradigm of hope, the second the paradigm of nostalgia, and the third the paradigm of indifference.

In classical antiquity, the paradigm of hope was almost entirely absent—the main exception being the Epicureans, who held that the world was still in a process of construction. The early Stoics followed a paradigm of indifference, claiming that history was simply a series of repeating cycles. Most of the classical writers followed the paradigm of nostalgia. That was the case of most Greek and Roman poets.[5]

In contrast, among Christians of the earliest generations, the paradigm of hope seems to have been dominant. Paul declares: "I consider that the sufferings of this present time are not worth comparing with the glory about to be revealed to us. For the creation waits with eager longing for the revealing of the children of God" (Rom. 8:18–19). The book of Revelation envisions a new heaven and a new earth. Justin and the apologists constantly refer to the hope of resurrection. Irenaeus divides history into four universal covenants or dispensations that lead to the covenant of Christ, to be followed by the final consummation.

The paradigm of the repetitive cycle does not seem to have had much allure for Christians, even though Origen, early in the third century, flirted with it,[6] and Augustine, late in the fourth, still felt the need to refute it.[7]

However, the paradigm of nostalgia, which was dominant in the cultures surrounding the church, slowly made its way into Christian thought. From the very beginning, Christians were persecuted because they were thought to be the cause of the various calamities that befell the Roman Empire. In the first century, Nero accused them of arson. By the second, it was commonly held that Christians were the cause of every disaster, for the gods were displeased at being abandoned in favor of the Christian God. Toward the end of that century, Tertullian responded to such charges by affirming that there had always been calamities, since long before Christians ever appeared in the world.[8] But by the third century, Cyprian, responding to similar charges made by Demetrian, proconsul of Africa, said:

> You impute it to the Christians that everything is decaying as the world grows old. What if old men should charge it on the Christians that they grow less strong in their old age; that they no longer, as formerly, have the same faculties, in the hearing of the ears, in the swiftness of their feet, in the keenness of their eyes, in the vigour of their strength, in the freshness of their organic powers, in the fullness of their limbs, and that although once the life of men endured beyond the age eight and nine hundred years, it can now scarcely attain to its hundredth year? We see grey hairs in boys–the hair fails before it begins to

grow; and life does not cease in old age, but it begins with old age. Thus, even at its very commencement, birth hastens to its close; thus, whatever is now born degenerates with the old age of the world itself; so that no one ought to wonder that everything begins to fail in the world, when the whole world itself is already in process of failing, and in its end.[9]

Augustine's Vision

Augustine supports this notion of the decadence and old age of the physical world by establishing a parallelism between the life stages of a human being and the ages of history. According to Augustine, human life comprises six stages:

> The first age, infancy, is spent in receiving bodily nourishment, and it is to be entirely forgotten when the person grows up. Then follows childhood, when we begin to have some memories. Adolescence then succeeds, when nature allows propagation of offspring and fatherhood. After adolescence comes young adulthood, which must take part in public duties and be brought under the laws...

> After the labours of young manhood, a little peace is given to old age. This takes him to an inferior age, lacking in luster, weak and more subject to disease, and it leads to death.[10]

In his commentary *On Genesis, against the Manicheans,* Augustine says that the days of creation are parallel to the ages of the world, which in turn are parallel to the ages of a human being. With this assertion he is probably drawing on what Seneca had said before, that the ages of human life were parallel to the ages of Roman history. But Augustine is now widening the scope of this assertion to include the entirety of history. (Lactantius, let it be said in passing, had earlier employed Seneca's scheme in order to claim that Rome, having reached senility, was about to disappear.[11]) According to Augustine, the first age or first day of history covers from Adam to Noah and is parallel to infancy "because our own infancy also disappears as in the flood." The second age is Abraham and is parallel to childhood. Then follow: the third, from Abraham to

David, which corresponds to adolescence; the fourth, from David to the exile, which is like young adulthood; the fifth, from the exile to the advent of Jesus Christ, which is like the "descent from young adulthood to old age"; the final, from Jesus Christ, corresponds to senility, and will end with the seventh age, which "will appear the morning when the Lord comes in the clarity of his power."[12]

In short, the world is old. Disasters and calamities should not surprise us. Even though we await a new heaven and new earth, the golden age of the physical creation is already past.

However, Augustine's vision of history is much wider than this, for in *The City of God* he develops an entire theory of the course of history as it follows two loves that have built two cities, the love of self, and the love of God. In this context, it is important to remember that for Augustine the term "city," *civitas,* is not simply an urban settlement, a place where people live together, but is much closer to what today we would call a "state." There are two different states, two orders, two systems of government, two citizenships. As Augustine himself explains it, "I divide the human race into two orders. The one consists of those who live according to man, and the other of those who live according to God."[13] The first group, those whose first love is for themselves, gives rise to the earthly city; the second group to the city of God. This does not mean that history has two clearly distinguishable entities, for the citizens of the city of God live in the midst of the earthly city and are hardly distinguishable from the rest. This may be seen in what Augustine says about the use of physical goods:

> But a household of men who do not live by faith strives to find an earthly peace in the goods and advantage which belong to this temporal life. By contrast, a household of men who live by faith looks forward to the blessings which are promised as eternal in the life to come; and such men make use of earthly and temporal things like pilgrims: they are not captivated by them, nor are they deflected by them from their progress towards God...
>
> Thus both kinds of men and both kinds of household make common use of those things which are necessary to this

mortal life; but each has its own very different end in using them.[14]

Eventually, according to Augustine, this distinction between two cities and two loves diminishes the importance of what takes place in the earthly city, or in the entire field of the temporal, for in the last analysis all that is really important is to belong to the city of God and eventually to live in it.

Augustine wrote *The City of God* because there were still pagans who did not accept the vision of Eusebius, that the history of Rome was also part of the history of Christianity. But in the end he seemed to conclude that the history of Rome was not all that important. If the pagans really wanted it, they could have it. Once again, Christian history was uninterested in secular history.

Orosius, Augustine's Popularizer

This may be seen in the work of Paulus Orosius, whose seven books on *History against the Pagans* were much more widely read during the Middle Ages than the quite bulky *City of God* of his teacher. What had led Augustine to write *City of God* was an accusation similar to the one made earlier by Demetrian against Cyprian: the great calamity of the fall of Rome before the Goths was due to Rome's having abandoned the gods that gave it power and having gone after the God of Christians. Although this was the main theme of Augustine's voluminous work, his argument was so far-reaching, and he dealt with so many different issues, that the refutation itself did not have the power it could. That is why Orosius, at the request of Augustine, decided to write a book to refute the notion that the fall of Rome was an unparalleled debacle and that Christians were responsible for it. Therefore, Orosius wished to show that long before the Empire became Christian there were already great calamities. And he did not miss an opportunity to do so with as many graphic details as he could!

The work consists of seven books, because that number had a profound significance for many Christians. Each of the books deals with a particular period in the history of Rome, and most of them are little more than a catalog of disasters, wars, plagues, and crimes. In spite of what pagans may now claim, Orosius declares, since the advent of Christianity such disasters have diminished; even the barbarians, influenced by Christianity, are now less violent.

Although he centers his attention on the history of Rome, Orosius does mention Babylon, Macedonia, and Carthage, particularly when comparing those ancient states with the Roman Empire serves to strengthen his argument. Thus, for instance, he claims that between the founding of Babylon and its fall to the Medes there were 1,164 years, which was exactly the same lapse of time as between the founding of Rome and its fall to the Goths.

In short, Orosius reads the history of all of humankind—or rather, of that portion of humankind within his own limited horizon—as a great drama directed by the divine providence. But it is directed not necessarily to the social well-being of humankind, to the just order of governments, or to the good use of the resources of the earth, but rather to the final salvation of those who by means of the knowledge of Jesus Christ have come to be part of the city of God.

This may be seen in the manner in which Orosius comments on the invasions of the barbarians and all the destruction and pain that these invasions brought with them:

> And yet, if the barbarians had been admitted into the territory of the Romans for this reason alone, because, in general, throughout the East and the West the churches of Christ were replete with Huns, Suevi, Vandals, and Burgundians, and with innumerable and different peoples of believers, the mercy of God would seem to be worthy of praise and to be extolled, since, even if with our own weakening, so many peoples would be receiving a knowledge of the truth which, surely, they could never have discovered except with this opportunity. For what loss is it to the Christian who is eager for eternal life to be taken away from this world at any time and by whatever means? Moreover, what gain is it to the pagan in the midst of Christians, obdurate against the faith, if he protracts his day a little longer, since he, whose conversion is despaired of, is destined to die?[15]

Precisely because he was interested only in the salvation of people, and because his desire was to show the calamities and atrocities of human history, Orosius wrote a book that later generations found fascinating. His *History against the Pagans,* which was in fact a religious interpretation of history, became the main text of "secular" history for the Middle Ages.

In short, in regard to basic texts on history, the people of the Middle Ages employed for church history the *Tripartite History* of Cassiodorus, which, as we have seen, was a continuation of the work of Eusebius, and, for secular history, the *History against the Pagans* of Orosius. Thus, a clear distinction was made between sacred history (as told by Cassiodorus) and secular history (as told by Orosius).

A Glance at the Middle Ages

The consequence of all this is that medieval church history has several characteristics that it derives in part from Eusebius and in part from Augustine and Orosius:

First, it is an ecclesiocentric history. Church history is not particularly interested in the history of humankind, except as a foreword or context for "sacred history." Actually, Sulpicius Severus (c.360–c.423) wrote a very elegant work in two books and 105 chapters that he called *Sacred History*. Of those chapters, eighty-one tell the story of the Hebrews up to Jesus Christ, five from Jesus to Constantine, and nineteen from Constantine to the year 400; but there is not one paragraph devoted to other peoples or traditions. Everything that Sulpicius Severus says is directly related to the biblical and ecclesiastical tradition. Political powers are mentioned only as they impinge on the life of Israel or the church. What we have here is a new and even stronger expression of the dichotomy between the sacred and the secular.

Second, even though one may claim to be writing the history of the church, in this entire tradition the church is in fact a suprahistorical reality. One may speak of a succession of bishops, of conflicts within the church, of varying relations with the state. But in truth the church cannot change. A bishop in the fifth century has to be the same as a bishop in the first. The order of worship cannot have changed. And most particularly, doctrines have to be immutable, for all these authors agree with the "doctrinalization" of Christianity that we found earlier in Justin and Eusebius.

Third, it often happens that in combining the two previous points, the church and its prestige come to be the final measure for every historical judgment. Sulpicius Severus shows this clearly.

He is only interested in so-called "secular" history when it directly affects the life of the church or of its forerunner, Israel. In other words, secular history has value only in function of sacred history.

Returning then to the simile of church history as a spiral, one can say that as the Middle Ages opened, the church was quite ready to claim for itself the Hebrew Scriptures, which it had already claimed in the first century; Greco-Roman philosophy, which it had begun to claim in the second century; the imperial tradition of Rome; and even the history of the states that had inherited the Roman Empire. But on this final point there is great hesitation, for the direction in which theology has developed makes it very difficult for the church to see how the political, economic, and social history of nations is part of the same sacred history to which it belongs. The church proclaims itself to be heir of the Hebrew tradition, of pagan philosophy, and of the Roman Empire, but it knows not what to do with that last political inheritance, beyond relegating it to the field of a supposedly "secular history."

9

The Struggle over the History
of the Church

Given the limitations of space, I cannot follow the history of church history through each of its developments. Therefore, in this chapter I look first at the period of the Reformation and the debate surrounding it in order to make some general comments about modern historiography. This prepares the way for the final chapter, in which I attempt to look at the future of history.

The Historiography of the Reformation

Much of the historical debate at the time of the Reformation had to do with the interpretation of Saint Augustine. At the very beginning, the nascent church had been forced to defend its right to use the Hebrew Scriptures. Several centuries later, when one of the leaders of that early struggle, Paul of Tarsus, had become an authoritative figure, there was a debate between Augustine and Pelagius regarding the proper interpretation of Paul. Now, at the time of the Reformation, there was a similar struggle regarding the interpretation of Augustine—and therefore, of Paul, and therefore, of the entirety of scripture. Thus, Luther and Calvin quoted those passages where Augustine spoke of salvation by the sole grace of God, while opponents quoted those other passages where Augustine says that grace gives us the power to do meritorious works.

However, the Reformation posed these questions within a much wider context. What was now being debated was not only the interpretation of Augustine, or even of Paul, but the entire corpus of Christian doctrine and practice. Therefore, the struggle for the inheritance of earlier Christian tradition could not be limited to a single point in that tradition, but had to include the entire history of the church.

In a word, what was at the center of the debate was whether the Western church, as it existed in the sixteenth century under the direction of the pope with its doctrines and practices, was a legitimate heir and continuation of the early church, or if, on the contrary, especially during its more recent history, the church had severed its connection with its own roots. According to the reformers, the difference between the church of their time and early Christianity was such that not only morality and practice, but even doctrine, worship, and church order had to be reformed. Those who remained faithful to the Roman Catholic Church underscored the historical continuity between the ancient church and the present, while the Protestants underscored the discontinuity between the two.

It is also helpful to point out, even in passing, that one of the main differences between the various Protestant groups was precisely the manner in which they understood that discontinuity between the ancient past and the present. Thus, for instance, for most of those commonly called "Anabaptist," discontinuity appeared very early—in many cases by the second century, and certainly by the time of Constantine. Furthermore, among those Anabaptists, many saw the entire history of the church from the second or the third century on as a great apostasy. Calvin and the Reformed tradition, like Luther and the Lutheran tradition, saw certain points of discontinuity from a fairly early date, but did not believe that there was an apostasy, but rather a deviation that had to be corrected. Thus, for instance, Calvin believed that the centralization of power in the person of the bishop of Rome was a great error and the cause of many evils, but even so he frequently quoted and followed the wisdom of Gregory the Great, whose pontificate was a milestone in the process of papal centralization. Luther, whose main concern was the matter of justification by grace, rued the way in which after Augustine's death the church had abandoned the doctrine of *sola gratia*. But he felt that the great detour had begun with scholasticism, which systematized and gave theological justification to the penitential system. For this reason he claimed that all the scholastic theologians were Pelagians, except Gregory of Rimini. In England, the tension between the more traditional Anglicans and the Puritans also had to do with their readings of history, for while some were ready to accept the customs and rites that had developed through the centuries, others insisted in purifying the church of everything that was not present in New Testament times.

However, the great debate was between Catholics and Protestants, for while the former held that the church as it existed in the sixteenth century was in full continuity with the church in previous centuries, the latter held that through the centuries there had been deviations that had to be corrected. This led to a continuing debate over the history of the church, in which the two great protagonists were, on the Protestant side, the *Centuries* of Magdeburg, and, on the Catholic side, the *Ecclesiastical Annals* of Baronius.

The *Centuries* of Magdeburg

Before the *Centuries,* several Protestant writings had attacked the Roman church, and more specifically the papacy, on the basis of historical research and claims. Such was *Life of the Roman Pontiffs,* written by ex-Augustinian Robert Barnes, and published in 1536 with a foreword by Luther. Also, Luther himself and several of his followers published various works in which they used history as an argument against the practices of the Roman church. However, all these efforts pale before the scope and ambition of the *Centuries* of Magdeburg.

The *Centuries* are a history of the church from a Lutheran perspective, prepared in Magdeburg by a group of scholars under the direction of Matthias Flacius Illyricus, and published in Basel between 1559 and 1574. Flacius was a leader of the most extreme faction within the Lutheran tradition. He believed that even

Melanchthon had wandered away from the truth discovered and proclaimed by Luther. He gathered in Magdeburg a group of scholars of similar convictions, who proposed to write an entire history of the church showing that Lutheranism was an affirmation of the best Christian tradition, and that Roman Catholicism was a significant departure from that tradition on various points, doctrinal as well as practical. Since the series devoted a volume to each century, it soon became known as the *Centuries.* The work did not go beyond the thirteenth century, for it was interrupted by the death of Flacius in 1575. But the thirteen volumes that had been published were a powerful political weapon against Catholicism, for they clearly showed that there was significant difference between the life of the church in its early centuries and what the Roman tradition held and practiced.

Flacius himself had written *Catalog of the Witnesses to Truth,* in which he collected quotations from four hundred different authors, all of them supposedly proving that from the beginnings of the Middle Ages the church began abandoning its former practices, and that several of the great saints of antiquity held positions similar to those of the Lutherans. But upon arriving at Magdeburg in 1549 he conceived the more ambitious project that resulted in the *Centuries.* As part of that project, he sent collaborators to several of the main libraries of Europe, where they collected data about the history of the church. Then, with a team of more than a dozen scholars, he began writing and publishing the great work.

The historical vision of the *Centuries* is clear and unabashed. The first volume includes practically an entire theology of the New Testament. The following volumes show the character of the ancient church and make abundant use of quotations from the most distinguished among the "fathers" of the church. Most of these quotes seem to contradict the various positions and practices of Roman Catholicism. For Flacius and his collaborators, as time went by, the papacy became increasingly opposed to true Christianity, and the most powerful and famous popes, such as Gregory VII and Innocent III, were in fact enemies of the true religion. This vision is supported with references to hundreds of ancient documents, and at the same time the credibility of the entire work is heightened by applying to those ancient documents the principles of historical criticism that were just being developed.

Although the *Centuries* were never completed, their impact was enormous, even more so since the work was well documented and much of its argument was based on quotations from some of the most respected writers of Christian antiquity. Already in 1571, when the great Magdeburg project was still in process, Pope Pius V named a commission to study the best way to respond to it; but the pope's death put an end to the works of the commission. Several Catholic authors attempted to refute the *Centuries,* arguing that they erred on one point or another, or writing brief histories that tried to show the continuity between the ancient church and the church of the sixteenth century. But none of them proved equal to the task.

The *Annals* of Baronius

It was precisely because of the challenge of the *Centuries* that the work of Baronius generally known as *Ecclesiastical Annals* had an enthusiastic response. Cesare Baronius was a scholar who had published a number of historical works, including important biographies of Saint Ambrose and Saint Gregory Nacianzen, as well as an extensive *Martyrologium.* Shortly after the publication of the first volume of the *Centuries,* Baronius became aware of the need to respond to them not with a mere refutation, but with an entirely different history of the church, written from a Catholic perspective and showing the continuity between the Roman practices of the sixteenth century and those of earlier generations. Like the Protestant historians in Magdeburg, Baronius determined to follow the rules of critical research so that his history could not be easily refuted on the basis of factual errors or because he gave excessive credence to a dubious document.

The first volume of the *Annals* appeared in 1588, fourteen years after the last volume of the *Centuries.* Its success was enormous and immediate. Soon an abridged and more popular edition was published in Italian. Two years later a similar abridgment appeared in German, then another in Polish. Even the Russian Orthodox Church, concerned as it was over the impact of Protestantism, produced its own version, in which it left out anything that was not compatible with Russian doctrine and practice.

Meanwhile, Baronius published volume after volume of his *Annals.* Since he had at his disposal the enormous resources of the

Vatican library, his work was as convincingly documented as the *Centuries*. Also, even before he published the first volume, several other historians had begun sending him materials and copies of manuscripts. When his fame expanded with the publication of the first volume, many more collaborated with him in this fashion. Eventually, Baronius was able to carry his *Annals* to the year 1198. Later others continued his work to 1565, so that the final edition has thirty-eight volumes. All this is an indication of the degree to which the controversies of the sixteenth century revolved around the question of who the true heirs of the ancient church were, just as the conflicts in the first century had revolved around the question of who the true heirs of the tradition of Israel were.

Modernity and Objectivity

Furthermore, ever since that time and well into the twentieth century the supposedly objective judgments that historians made about both the *Centuries* and the *Annals* show that the conflict continued. For instance, a Protestant historian says:

> However poor was the work of the authors of the Magdeburg Centuries, they were at least honest in arraying their sources. This is more than can be said of Caesar Baronius, whose *Annales Ecclesiastici* was the official Catholic counterblast to the Protestant work. Whereas his criticism is no whit better than theirs, he adopted the cunning policy, unfortunately widely obtaining since his day, of simply ignoring or suppressing unpleasant facts, rather than of refuting the inferences drawn from them. His talent for switching the attention to a side-issue, and for tangling instead of clearing problems, made the Protestants justly regard him as "a great deceiver."[1]

But the same sort of criticism is raised by Catholic historians regarding the *Centuries* of Magdeburg. Commenting on that work, a Spanish Catholic author in the middle of the twentieth century declared that:

> The passionate approach which is characteristic of this entire work and seriously detracts from its objective and historical value had the immediate effect of awakening among Catholics a desire for study and research, with the

purpose of refuting that collection of baseless affirmations and imputations with actual historical facts.

Almost immediately he comments on the work of Baronius:

This was truly a fundamental work, composed with a critical sense and an objectivity that were much greater than those of the *Centuriators,* and which therefore has an immeasurable historical value. It is true that it also suffers from its apologetic tendency; but it is impossible to value properly the merit of having collected an enormous number of historical sources of the first order, which his work usually quotes extensively.[2]

What is most remarkable in comparing these two evaluations is that both acknowledge the defects of both works. But while the Protestant says that the defects of Baronius are greater, the Catholic judges things otherwise.

With these two examples, one written in 1920 and the other in 1967, we come to the next stage of our history of church history. Significantly, the Protestant author accuses Baronius of not being sufficiently objective, while the Catholic says that he is. We therefore find ourselves at a time when the main criterion for judging the value of a historical work is its objectivity. It is interesting to note that these two authors reflect their own confessional perspective in their supposedly objective judgments. The Protestant author affirms quite objectively that the *Centuries* are more objective than the works of Baronius. With the same objectivity, his Catholic counterpart affirms the contrary.

The nineteenth and twentieth centuries were the time when objectivity reached the status of main criterion for evaluation, not only in the historical sciences but in every other discipline. In the field of general history, probably the most influential author was Leopold von Ranke, who in 1828, in an appendix to his vast *History of the Romanic and Germanic Peoples,* developed an entire program for historical research. In that appendix, von Ranke insists on the need for a critical study of documents and other historical sources, but he adds also that such critical study must take into account the atmosphere or context in which each document was formed, as well as the tendencies, purposes, and prejudices of those who wrote each document. Von Ranke suggests that taking this into account, and abandoning every prejudice, a modern historian must tell events "just as they happened."

This historical science, like any science, must be universal. Von Ranke himself offered an example of this, for after writing his *History of the Romanic and Germanic People* and many other works, such as his famous *History of the Popes,* he began writing *Universal History,* which was interrupted by his death and which his disciples eventually brought up to the fifteenth century. His dream was to apply his method of objective inquiry to the entirety of human history.

These two characteristics of history as von Ranke conceived it, objectivity and universality, are a reflection of the values that took hold of the European mind and that were called "modern." The modern ideal for knowledge had been admirably summarized much earlier by René Descartes in his *Discourse on Method.* His famous all-encompassing doubt was simply a means to make certain that what he would in the end affirm as knowledge would be absolutely indubitable, so that no one could accuse the researcher of having been carried away by feelings, imagination, prejudice, or any other subjective element. The doubt of Descartes is not based on the premise that it is impossible to know something with absolute certainty, as in the case of the skeptics, but exactly the opposite. It is based on the premise that true knowledge is objective and that any knowledge that is not absolutely indubitable, without any possibility of subjective prejudice, is unworthy of the name of knowledge.

Such objectivity is parallel to universality. Descartes himself begins his *Discourse on Method* by declaring that:

> Good sense is mankind's most equitably divided endowment, for everyone thinks that he is so abundantly provided with it that even those with the most insatiable appetites and most difficult to please in other ways do not usually want more than they have of this...[I]t is the only thing which makes us men and distinguishes us from animals, and I am therefore satisfied that it is fully present in everyone of us.[3]

What this means is that reason, as Descartes understands it, is the same everywhere and in every circumstance, and therefore, if something is proven by pure reason, without allowing any room for personal, social, or cultural considerations, that demonstration will be universally valid. Since it is reason or common sense that distinguishes the human being from animals, every rational human being is able to acknowledge the truth of what Descartes affirms as he emerges from his methodological doubt.

The same idea becomes increasingly dominant among historians–and specifically, church historians–during modernity, even though many do not leave behind the polemical purposes that may be noted in the two authors quoted above, commenting on the *Centuries* of Magdeburg and the *Ecclesiastical Annals* of Baronius. It was generally held that "serious" history should be totally objective, and this to such a point that even history written with polemical purposes was only valid if it was dressed in objectivity. Thus, it was said that the main task of history was to present events as they happened, and even to read them with such an objectivity that the historian understood them better than those who lived through them. Furthermore, thanks to the impact of the physical sciences, there was a strong insistence that history was a science, and that as such its purpose was to discover the laws that govern historical events–or even better, to discover the law that binds together all those events, much as the law of gravity binds the universe together. In brief, history being a science, it was to be interested first of all in the "facts," and, behind the facts, in the laws governing them.[4]

In that context of modernity all theological sciences, if they were to claim the title of "sciences," had to be subject to the same criteria of rationality, objectivity, and universality that ruled in other sciences. If in the field of physics, for instance, what is to be affirmed is only what can be objectively proven in a laboratory and can be universally tested by any observer free of prejudice, the same criterion is to be applied to theology, biblical studies, church history, and so on. Theology, which in the thirteenth century had given birth to universities, in the nineteenth found itself forced to defend its right to remain in the university. Significantly, all the great theological systems of the nineteenth century were apologetic; part of their purpose was to show the intellectual respectability of theology and of Christian faith.

Even among those who did not allow themselves to be carried away by the emphasis on objectivity, insisting that in order to know the history of the church one has to be a part of the church itself and to experience its faith and its life, there always remained an apologetic tone. In this sense, there is a remarkable parallelism between the purposes of Origen in arguing that Christianity is the true philosophy, and those of Schleiermacher in basing religion on the "feeling of dependence," or of Ritschl in basing it on moral values. Besieged by the "rational," "objective," and "universal" sciences, theology found itself in an intellectual corner, and struggled mightily to find a new place within intellectual discourse.

The Legacy of Modernity

Even though today much of this has been left behind, and even though today we may critique modernity's false presuppositions, it is important to underscore that, at least in the field of church history, the modern spirit has bequeathed us a valuable inheritance. Thanks to the modern emphasis on demonstrable objectivity, historical studies had to develop criteria in order to judge the value of documents and other historical sources. This conglomerate of criteria, commonly called the "historical critical method," had its impact on biblical studies by posing questions regarding the date, composition, authorship, and purpose of the books of the Bible. This is so well known that there is no need to insist on it. But what we often forget is that throughout the nineteenth century and much of the twentieth the study of church history followed the same route. Before being employed as a source for historical knowledge, every ancient or medieval text had to be subjected to an intense historical critical scrutiny.

The work of those historians was simply monumental. What biblical scholars did with the twenty-seven books of the New Testament, these historians of the nineteenth and early twentieth centuries did with hundreds of patristic texts that had been known since antiquity, as well as with several dozen others that had been lost and were rediscovered at the time.

Particularly remarkable was the work of the prince of church historians in the modern age, Adolf von Harnack. Although he was not able to complete it in his life time, his *History of Christian Literature up to Eusebius–Geschichte des altchristliche Literatur bis Eusebius*–applies the historical critical method to practically every text studied. Jointly with other colleagues, Harnack founded the series *Texts and Investigations on the History of Ancient Christian Literature–Texte und Untersuchungen zur Geschichte der altchristlichen Literatur*–and contributed to that series no fewer than forty-nine monographs. To this day, before employing any ancient text, historians inquire what Harnack had to say about it.

Beyond Objectivity

Even having acknowledged the value of the historical critical method and its contribution to historical studies, it is necessary to acknowledge also that its supposed objectivity is little more than supposed.

Harnack himself was convinced that the history of Christian theology during the early centuries, leading to the formulation of dogma in the great ecumenical councils, had been a process whereby the simple teachings of Jesus were Hellenized and complicated, eventually leading to the deification of Jesus himself. What happened during the Protestant Reformation was the beginning of a process of depuration, ridding Christianity of all that had been added through the centuries. But that process was incomplete, for the reformers did not understand that the gospel as they had learned it and as they continued teaching it was simply a Hellenization of the simple original message of Jesus. Now, by means of the historical critical method, it would be possible to continue that process of depuration, and to rediscover the original message of Jesus.

Although that is the main thrust of Harnack's extensive *History of Dogma–Lehrbuch der Dogmengeschichte*–where it is most clearly expressed is in a series of lectures he published in 1900 under the title of *What Is Christianity?–Das Wesen des Christentums*. In the third lecture, Harnack defines original Christianity as being summarized under three heads:

> Firstly, The Kingdom of God and its Coming.
>
> Secondly, God the Father and the Infinite Value of the Human Soul.
>
> Thirdly, The Higher Righteousness and the Commandment of Love.[5]

After commenting on each of these three points, Harnack passes judgment on each of the main bodies of Christianity. About Greek Orthodoxy, he declares that "it takes the form, not of a Christian product in Greek dress, but of a Greek product in Christian dress."[6]

His judgment on Roman Catholicism is even more severe:

What qualifications has the gospel here undergone, and how much of it is left? Well—this is not a matter that needs many words—the whole outward and visible institution of a Church claiming divine dignity has no foundation whatever in the gospel. It is a case, not of distortion, but of total perversion[7]

Roman Catholicism has nothing to do with the gospel, nay, is in fundamental contradiction with it.[8]

In contrast to that judgment, Harnack's evaluation of Protestantism is quite positive:

Anyone who looks at the external condition of Protestantism, especially in Germany, may, at first sight, well exclaim: "What a miserable spectacle!" But no one can survey the history of Europe from the second century to the present time without being forced to the conclusion that in the whole course of this history the greatest movement and the one most pregnant with good was the Reformation in the sixteenth century; even the great change which took place at the transition to the nineteenth is inferior to it in importance. What do all our discoveries and inventions and our advances in outward civilization signify in comparison with the fact that today there are thirty millions of Germans, and many more millions of Christians outside Germany, who possess a religion without priests, without sacrifices, without "fragments" of grace, without ceremonies—a spiritual religion![9]

All this is given here as a remarkable example of the contradiction between the pretended objectivity of modern historiography and what in fact such historiography offers. Harnack, the most distinguished historian of his time, well versed in the historical critical method, and champion of scientific objectivity, interprets Christianity and its entire history with prejudices typical of the German intelligentsia of the late nineteenth and early twentieth centuries.

In his summary of the message of Jesus, Harnack underscores "the infinite value of the human soul." As he explains his point, it becomes clear that this has to do with the individual soul and that Harnack's interpretation of faith bears the mark of modernity with its emphasis on individuality. There is not a single ancient Christian document, neither in the New Testament nor beyond it, which speaks of the infinite value of the human soul, and much less of such a value as one of the three main pillars of Christianity. His comments on Greek Orthodoxy and Roman Catholicism are no more objective, and clearly reflect his own position as a German Protestant at the turn of the century. He even claims that the purpose of Jesus was to "destroy" the sort of religion that existed among Jews, and that Judaism is much less important in the original sayings of Jesus than is often thought. In so saying, he reflects the growing German anti-Semitism that would later have dire consequences. His interpretation of the Protestant Reformation would surprise Luther himself, who probably would not be able to understand how Harnack's religion was the result of the Lutheran Reformation. And to cap it off, everything is seen from a strictly German perspective, which makes it appear that the most remarkable fact in the history of the church is that the new faith now has thirty million German followers.

All this is summarized by Harnack himself in claiming that true Christianity is "a spiritual religion"–and what Harnack understands by "spiritual" is that it is reasonable, progressive, modern.

Summary and Conclusion

The modern age began with a struggle over who would claim possession of the history of the church. Both Luther and his opponents claimed for themselves the best and the most ancient of that history. The Lutheran historians at Magdeburg and their opponent Baronius continued the same struggle. Although one would expect that modernity, with its emphasis on objectivity, would make the conflict less intense and passionate, what actually happened was exactly the opposite, for Roman Catholicism tended to see modernity as a great enemy, whereas Protestant liberalism saw in it the victory of the Protestant spirit. Thus, while Pius IX was issuing his *Syllabus of Errors,* with a list of supposed errors that today shock us for their reactionary spirit, liberal German theologians on the Protestant side were seeking to show that modernity was the outcome and the best ally of Protestantism. Many, such as Harnack, seemed to believe that anything to be found in the gospel that could not be reconciled with the spirit of modernity was to be discarded.

In consequence, precisely at the time that the value of objectivity was most loudly proclaimed by church historians, those very historians were divided in two camps. In the Roman Catholic camp, much of what was being written was a mere continuation of the arguments and interpretations of Baronius, for going beyond that seemed to be a capitulation to the spirit of modernity. In the other camp, the Protestant side, historians such as Harnack believed themselves to be absolutely objective, even though today it is quite clear that their supposed objectivity was little more than the common subjectivity of the intellectual bourgeoisie of Germany at the time.

This left still pending the great question debated by the Centuriators at Magdeburg and by Baronius: whose is the history of the church? And not only was that question still unresolved; there was another even more difficult question, namely, what future can there be for the history of the church if even such scholarly efforts as those of Harnack and his contemporaries show the limitations of their perspectives?

10

The Future of Church History

No matter how much historians might claim that they are studying the past objectively, the fact is that all historians must necessarily look at the past from their own perspectives, from the points at which that very history has placed them. Furthermore, the perspective of a historian is not only a matter of the present moment but also of the vision of the future from which history is studied and written. Thus, after a brief summary about various ways in which some past historians saw the future, this chapter explores and tries to express the vision of the future from which I write history today, and invites others to do likewise.

Past Visions of the Future

When Eusebius wrote his *Church History,* his vision of the future was mostly one of the continuation and amplification of the new order that Constantine had inaugurated. Eusebius still had an eschatological expectation, but that expectation was pushed to the background, and meanwhile he expected the Roman Empire, now joined to the Christian church, to continue prospering for the benefit both of the Empire and of the church.

When slightly more than a century later Augustine wrote his *City of God,* while he shared Eusebius' postponed eschatology, he did not believe that the Empire would continue progressing. Not only had Rome fallen before the advance of the Goths but Augustine was convinced that the history of the various incarnations of the "earthly city," including Rome, was not of much significance. The future that Eusebius saw was tied to the Roman Empire. The future that Augustine saw did not have any such bonds, either to that empire nor to any other political order.

The vision of Gregory of Tours was quite different, for his *History of the Franks* saw in the various Germanic kingdoms, and particularly in the Frankish kingdom, the continuation of the Roman Empire, and therefore restored to secular history an importance it seemed to have lost with Saint Augustine. (And let it be said in passing that the future that Gregory foresaw was partly fulfilled when, in the year 800, slightly more than two centuries after the death of Gregory, Charlemagne was crowned Emperor of the West. Furthermore, partially because of that vision of the future on the part of Gregory, Jordanes, and other Germanic historians, that dream of the continuation of the old Roman Empire lived on at least until the first half of the twentieth century, when there were still European rulers who claimed to be heirs to the throne of the Caesars.)

When in the nineteenth century modern historians such as Harnack and his colleagues told the story of the ancient church, their vision of the future was typically modern: humanity would continue advancing in an almost inevitable progress, and this would lead to an age of greater understanding and critical objectivity, leaving aside all the "superstitions" of former times. Reason would rule over emotion and prejudice. The critical study of the past would produce a form of Christianity ever purer, more rational, less superstitious. Jointly with Christianity, Western civilization would impose its sway over the rest of the world, creating a global civilization ever more prosperous, more just, more promising.

History is read differently from each of these perspectives. From the perspective of Eusebius, the political history of the Roman Empire is read as a preparation for the new age of collaboration between church and state. From the perspective of Augustine, that political history is simply one more example of the futility of the "earthly city." From the perspective of Gregory of Tours, what began in the times of Eusebius and Constantine continues in the kingdom of the Franks. From the point of view of historians in the nineteenth century, the history of the church and of its doctrines is the story of how the gospel of Jesus, originally simple and rational, became increasingly complicated as it adapted to the complexities of antiquity, and how now, with modern discoveries and modern objectivity, we are moving toward a better understanding of God's eternal plan, and toward its fulfillment.

All this should suffice to show that the "future" from which church history is read and written has a profound impact on the contents and interpretation of that history.

Thus, the "future of history" has a twofold meaning. In the first sense, we are asking what direction history will take in the coming generations. In the second sense, we must also ask what vision of the future gives form and content to our present research and interpretation of history. While these two are intertwined, it is important to remember both of them, so as not to forget that the "future" from which we write is not only an attempt to glimpse what the future will bring, but also affects, sometimes even unwittingly, the manner in which we describe the past.

From What Future Do We Read the Past?

For these reasons it is of paramount importance for historians today to say something about the future that we expect. We do not speak of such a future claiming that somehow our historical knowledge provides us with a crystal ball where we can see events before they unfold. The various futures that the historians studied in this book thought they could foresee have only become partially true, and many have shown to be false. Therefore, if there is something that we must learn from the very rapid overview in this book of the history of church history, that is that our visions of the future are no more than working hypotheses—necessary, reasonable, well thought out hypotheses, but even so, still hypothetical.

On the other hand, this does not mean that history should not try to look at the future. Certainly, the main reason throughout the ages that people have studied the past is in order to predict the future—not to foretell all its details, but to know what we are to expect, what may be the result of certain actions, and so on. The ancient Egyptians' keeping registers of the floods of the Nile—their dates, levels, and so forth—was at least in part in order to be able to foretell the dates, levels, and consequences of future floods. The ancient Romans' writing in their annals the events of each year was so that such experiences would serve as political instruction for future generations, helping them to govern the city well.

The same is true of church history. If at various times Christians have looked at their own past, they have done so having in mind their present struggles and the future form of the church and its doctrines. Thus, for instance, when the author of Ephesians tells his readers that they are to be "built upon the foundation of the apostles and prophets" (Eph. 2:20), he is reading that ancient history of the prophets and the apostles as a guide for the future life of his readers. When the bishops gathered in Chalcedon in the year 451 and began their "Definition of Faith" with the words "following therefore the holy fathers we all teach with one voice," what they did was to reclaim the ancient story of their ancestors in the faith in order to determine that neither Nestorianism nor Monophysism would have a place in the future church. When in Magdeburg Matthias Flacius and his companions wrote their *Centuries,* and when in Rome Baronius wrote his *Annals,* each of them was reading the history of past centuries as a way to describe and determine the shape that the church would take in the future. And when I wrote *A History of Christian Thought*[1] and *The Story of Christianity,*[2] I did so with an agenda toward the future, in the first case without even knowing it myself, and in the second case with full consciousness of the fact.

In summary, even though in university classrooms we may be told that we study history with the sole purpose of knowing the past, the truth is that no matter whether we know it or not, no matter whether we confess it or not, we study history because we believe that it somehow illumines our present and announces our future.

An Encompassing Future

From what future then should church history be studied today? In answer to that question, I believe three points should be underlined.

In the first place, we must remember that probably the most important event that has taken place in the story of Christianity in the last two hundred years is the church's becoming for the first time universal. What I referred to when speaking of the "changing cartography of church history" is part of the future from which church history must now be written.

This means that it is no longer possible to tell the story of the church as if its culmination were the forms that it has taken in the North Atlantic, be they Catholic or Protestant forms. All the textbooks that I studied in my youth were written from that perspective. Those written in the United States implied that all previous history led toward North American Protestantism. The same was done, *mutatis mutandis,* by Catholic historians in France or in Italy, as well by Protestants in Germany or Great Britain.

Today I read those books and am surprised at having studied and recommended them, not only in the United States and in Europe but also in some of the best institutions in Latin America. What is surprising is not that they were written. After all, all historians must write from their own perspective and for their own public. What is surprising is that I read, translated, and recommended them as if they were truly mine, as if their visions of history did not marginalize a growing number of believers, or even worse, as if the marginalization that we suffered were logical, natural, and acceptable.

Today, as indicated in chapters 1 and 2 of this book, history must be written taking into consideration the cartographic and topographic changes that have taken place in the life of the church and its leadership.

A consequence of this is that we shall have to set aside the old division between "church history" and the "history of missions." When I studied for my doctorate in one of the most prestigious universities of the world, that distinction was basic in the curriculum. As a result, that university granted me a doctorate in historical theology without ever once asking me if I knew anything about the history of the church and its theology in China, in India, in Armenia, or even in my native Cuba.

My ignorance of the history of worldwide Christianity was revealed to me when, around the year 1962, a commission in Buenos Aires that was preparing textbooks for theological education asked me to write a history of missions. The process of writing that book made me recognize how much of the history of the worldwide church I did not know. It made it increasingly apparent that history as I had studied it was not the way I should write it. Today, when that history of missions that I wrote in the sixties has been out of print for more than thirty years, I have agreed to produce a new edition with the collaboration of a friend who is a missiologist. Both he and I are convinced, and will clearly state in our introduction, that the book itself is quite provisional and that our intention is not to continue promoting the history of missions as a separate discipline, but rather to remind our colleagues that the story of Christianity involves much more than the Mediterranean or the North Atlantic basins. When history is written from China, it can no longer be written as if the work of Alopen and the Nestorians of the seventh century, that of Matteo Ricci in the late sixteenth and early seventeenth, that of the Catholicism that existed there ever since that date, and that of Protestantism that arrived in the nineteenth century were not part of the history of the church, but only of a marginal "history of missions." All of this I have made clear in earlier chapters of this book, to the point of speaking of the "cataclysmic changes" that are taking place in the history of the church.

A Truly Catholic Future

The second point that I believe to be characteristic of the future from which history must be written today is diversity and inclusivity in matters of gender, class, culture, and race. Until recently, those who wrote the history of the church were, with few exceptions, white European or white North American males. In discussing the "changing topography" of church history, I have given some indication of what this different future implies for the present reading and writing of church history.

What all this means is that the future of the history of the church—that is, the future that I now imagine when I think of the coming generations and that therefore impacts the manner in which I read the past—is not only universal but also catholic. I have already explained in the chapter "Mapping a New Catholicity" how those two words that we usually take to be equivalent—*universal* and *catholic*—are in many ways different and even opposed. True catholicity requires unity within diversity. Therefore, in declaring that the future of the church is "catholic," what I mean is that the church will be increasingly diverse and will have to find ways to experience and express its unity within that diversity, and to read its history from an enormous variety of perspectives.

Because it will be written by people in various parts of the world–Chinese, Russians, Poles, Mexicans, Nigerians, men and women, sociologists, psychologists, Catholics, Protestants, and on and on–the history of the church in the future will have to be not only universal but also catholic. And since no one can write such a history alone, it will have to be, like the very catholicity of the church, a constant dialogue and mutual correction.

A Future of Marginalized Incarnation

Third, the future from which I write the history of the church is one of marginalized incarnation. Ever since Eusebius wrote his *Church History,* the church has been at the centers of power and prestige. Constantine supported it. Theodosius made it the official religion of the state. When in the times of Augustine the political center crumbled before the Germanic invasions, Augustine reinterpreted history, so that the city of God, precisely because it was God's, could leave aside the vicissitudes of the earthly city and still remain at the center. Ever since, the church has been inclined to choose between those two paradigms, depending on the situation in which it finds itself–but always remaining at the center.

In most cases, particularly in the North Atlantic, the church has followed the first of these two paradigms, that of Eusebius, placing itself at the center of political power, supporting it, and having it support the church. This was true in times of Constantine and Theodosius. This was true in the various Germanic kingdoms as they became Christian. This was true throughout most of the history of the Greek church, the Russian church, and the Roman church. This was true in most Protestant countries. In the Protestant lands of Switzerland, Germany, Scandinavia, England, and Scotland, Protestantism flourished under the wing of the state. Meanwhile, in the Catholic countries of Europe and in their colonies in Latin America and other parts of the world, Roman

Catholicism did likewise. The same has happened, at least until a relatively recent time, even in a number of countries in which the separation of church and state became a matter of law. In Mexico, in spite of that separation, cultural and social pressures have favored and still favor Roman Catholicism, even though the state is officially secular. The same is true–though to a lesser degree–of Protestantism in the United States. Here, until the times of Kennedy, it was taken for granted that the President would belong to a Protestant church. In all this, the paradigm of Eusebius has ruled.

The other paradigm, that of Augustine, has been attractive whenever for some reason the church and Christians have not been able to place themselves at the center of power–political, cultural, and economic. In the case of Augustine, the reason for this was that the center of political power had collapsed. In many other cases, the center has been hostile or indifferent, and then Christians have told themselves that this was not important, because after all they belonged to the city of God, and the civil power is part of the earthly city that is to pass. This was the attitude of the Monophysites in Egypt until the Arab conquest freed them from the Byzantine yoke, and remained their attitude when the Arab regime turned out to be an even more confining yoke. That was the attitude of the Albigensians of Southern France when Innocent III unleashed against them the fury of the Crusades. Such was the attitude of the Anabaptists of the sixteenth century when Catholics as well as Protestants declared them heretics. Such was the attitude of most Latin American Protestants when we were told that being Latin American meant being Catholic, or when we were oppressed and even persecuted officially or extraofficially. In all these cases, those who are marginalized have been attracted by the paradigm of Augustine, which implies that civil power is a matter of interest to the earthly city, but not really to the city of God.

Today it should be clear that these paradigms must change. There are few places remaining in the world where the state supports the church–and even those are disappearing. The process, apparently irreversible, is neither easy nor direct. There are still among Roman Catholics those who speak of a "new Christendom." As a strange and sad anomaly, it is interesting to note that among some Latin American Protestants who until recently followed the paradigm of Augustine as a way of understanding their political and social marginality, today the paradigm of Eusebius seems to be gaining credence. Thus, there are Protestants who are proud that members of their churches are in government and who celebrate this, not because such people promote just or better laws, but simply because they are "ours." Significantly, the same is happening in the United States, where some groups that until a few years ago insisted that Christianity had nothing to do with politics, today celebrate and proclaim their contacts with senators and with the President.

That easy shift from one paradigm to another shows that even though the two seem very different, at bottom they have an important common characteristic: they are both triumphalist. One places the church and believers at the center by joining them to the political, cultural, and economic center. The other places them at the center by spiritualizing reality and convincing them that after all, the social and political reality is not all that important.

As an alternative to these two paradigms, I like to think that the future of the church will be one of incarnate marginality. It is from that vision of the church that today I write and interpret the history of the church, being quite conscious that, as any vision of the future, this is no more than a working hypothesis, with a measure of utopia and a large measure of personal preference, but I believe also with some basis in reality.

When I speak of incarnate marginality, what I mean above all is that Christians must acknowledge that our proper place, both as individuals and as the church, is not necessarily at the center. Without condemning Eusebius or Constantine, without declaring the entire Middle Ages apostate, without rejecting the inheritance that we have received from so many centuries of official and extraofficial support by the state and society at large, we must affirm that the proper place for those who follow Jesus Christ is the margin rather than the center; it is the valley rather than the hilltop; it is the cross rather than the throne.

Quite probably, in the near future such marginality will be imposed on us by circumstances. We can already see how churches in general are losing their influence in political spheres, in the higher social circles, in the mass media, and in general in all the centers of power. In several traditionally Christian countries, those who believe in Jesus Christ share the same space and political order today with Muslims, Buddhists, Hindus, atheists, and others. No longer can the church claim the religious hegemony it once had, but rather, it is forced to enter into interreligious dialogue, and to do this with ever fewer political, cultural, or social props. Many Christians think that this means that the church is losing its power, and yearn with nostalgia for the old times of Christendom. But if I understand correctly the message of Jesus, that marginality, whether imposed or voluntary, is to be received as an opportunity to recover an essential dimension of that message:

> "The kings of the Gentiles lord it over them; and those in authority over them are called benefactors. But not so with you; rather the greatest among you must become like the youngest, and the leader like one who serves." (Lk. 22:25–26)

The church of the future, that catholic and universal church that I have just described, will be a church of service, but of service from the margin. It will not be the church at the center, as in the paradigm of Eusebius. Its great temptation will be to become a purely spiritual church, claiming to be above the vicissitudes of human history, as in the paradigm of Augustine. However, if it is obedient to the gospel of Jesus Christ, it will be a church incarnate, present, a participant of human life, but present above all at the margins, without pretending or even seeking to be at the center or to control, and with a clear call of service to all humankind.

Notes

Chapter 1: The Changing Cartography

[1]David B. Barrett et al., *World Christian Encyclopedia* (Oxford: University Press, 2001), 2:14–15; table 1-4.

[2]Williston Walker, *A History of the Christian Church*, rev. Cyril C. Richardson, Wilhelm Pauck, and Robert T. Handy (New York: Charles Scribner's Sons, 1959).

[3]Henri Pirenne, *Mohammed and Charlemagne* (Cleveland: World Publishing Company, 1957), 284–85.

[4]Kenneth Scott Latourette, *A History of the Expansion of Christianity*, vol. 4, *The Great Century in Europe and the United States of America: A.D. 1800–A.D. 1914* (New York: Harper & Brothers, 1941), 13.

[5]Ibid., 21.

Chapter 2: The Changing Topography

[1]I shall discuss the postmodern challenge to the history of Christianity in chapter 4.

[2]Kenneth Scott Latourette, *A History of Christianity* (New York: Harper & Brothers, 1953).

[3]I shall return to this thought in chapter 7.

[4]More will be said on the Centuriators of Magdeburg and on Baronius in chapter 9.

[5]I have discussed this more fully elsewhere: *Faith and Wealth: A History of Early Church Ideas on the Origin, Significance, and Use of Money* (San Francisco: Harper & Row, 1990), and *Mañana: Christian Theology from a Hispanic Perspective* (Nashville: Abingdon Press, 1990), 101–15.

[6]Paula E. Buford, "The Lost Tradition of Women Pastoral Caregivers from 1925 to 1967" (Ph.D. diss., Columbia Theological Seminary, Decatur, Georgia, 1997).

[7]Two books with abundant examples of women historians working on the daily life of medieval women are Susan Mosher Stuard, ed., *Women in Medieval Society* (Philadelphia: University of Pennsylvania Press, 1976), and Mary Erler and Maryanne Kowaleski, eds., *Women & Power in the Middle Ages* (Athens, Ga.: University of Georgia Press, 1988).

[8]Leo G. Perdue correctly warns his readers against such oversimplifications: "To concentrate primarily on the content of history means that much of the Old Testament is either ignored or slighted. This is particularly true of texts and traditions in which creation plays a prominent role," *The Collapse of History* (Minneapolis: Fortress Press, 1994), 113.

[9]An example of the work that is now possible on daily life in Egypt, thanks to the new interest on the subject as well as to the recovery of papyri, is Naphtali Lewis, *Life in Egypt under Roman Rule* (Oxford: Clarendon, 1983).

[10]Good examples are Georges Duby, *L'économie rurale et la vie des campagnes dans l'occident médiéval* (Paris: Aubier, 1962); Robert Fossier, *Paysans d'Occident (XIᵉ-XIVᵉ siècles)*, (Paris: Presses Universitaires de France, 1984); Michel Mollat, *The Poor in the Middle Ages: An Essay in Social History* (New Haven, Conn.: Yale University Press, 1986); Werner Rösener, *Peasants in the Middle Ages* (Urbana: University of Illinois Press, 1992).

[11]See, for instance, Kenneth Scott Latourette, *A History of the Expansion of Christianity*, vol. 4, *The Great Century in Northern Africa and Asia* (New York: Harper & Brothers, 1944), 406.

[12]Adolph von Harnack, *History of Dogma*, vol. 5 (New York: Russell and Russell, 1958), 262.

[13]Orlando O. Espín, *The Faith of the People: Theological Reflections on Popular Catholicism* (Maryknoll, N.Y.: Orbis, 1997), 113.

[14]Sydney E. Ahlstrom, *A Religious History of the American People*, vol. 2 (Garden City, N.Y.: Doubleday, 1975), 84.

Chapter 3: Cataclysmic Changes

[1]I shall return to Eusebius, and deal more concretely with his impact on the content of early church history, in chapter 7.

[2]Zaida Maldonado Pérez, "The Subversive Dimensions of the Visions of the Martyrs of the Roman Empire of the Second through Early Fourth Centuries," (Ph.D. diss., Saint Louis University, Saint Louis, 1999).

[3]*Book of Common Worship* (Louisville: Westminster/John Knox Press, 1993), 407.

[4]*The United Methodist Hymnal: Book of United Methodist Worship* (Nashville: The United Methodist Publishing House, 1989), 34.

[5]One point at which many Christians today are still impacted by the tensions engendered by that situation is the common use of the Apostles' Creed among Western Christians. This stems from the controversy over the *filioque* clause that had been added in the West–probably in Spain–to the ancient Nicene Creed. In the royal chapel at Aachen, and generally throughout the West, it was affirmed that the Holy Spirit proceeds from the Father *and the Son–filioque*. The East objected to this unauthorized interpolation in the Creed. In the heat of controversy, each side declared that the other was heretical. As a way to avoid taking sides, the popes and others began to promote the ancient Roman Creed–or Old Roman Symbol–and to claim that it had come from the apostles themselves. Eventually, this formula–now called the Apostles' Creed–became more common in the West than the Nicene Creed.

[6]Although Pirenne had published his view earlier in a number of articles and essays, his major work *Mohammed and Charlemagne* was published after his death in 1935. It was first published in English in 1939 (London: G. Allen & Unwin).

[7]Williston Walker, *A History of the Christian Church*, rev. Cyril C. Richardson, Wilhelm Pauck, and Robert T. Handy (New York: Charles Scribner's Sons, 1959), 145.

[8]Henrici Denzinger, *Enchiridion Symbolorum: Definitionum et declarationum de rebus fidei et morum*, 31st ed. (Rome: Herder, 1950), 490.

Chapter 4: The Failing Map of Modernity

[1]Frédéric Hoffet, *L'impérialisme protestant: Considérations sur le destin inégal des peuples protestants et catholiques dans le monde actuel* (Paris: Flamarion, 1948).

[2]René Descartes, *Discourse on Method and Meditations,* trans. Laurence J. Lafleur (Indianapolis: Bobbs-Merrill, 1960), 15.

[3]José Ortega y Gasset, *Historia como sistema,* in *Obras completas* (Madrid: Revista de Occidente, 1947), 6:16.

[4]Ashis Nandy, *The Intimate Enemy: Loss and Recovery of Self under Colonialism* (Delhi: Oxford Press, 1983), xiv. Quoted by Stephen Slemon, "Modernism's Last Post," in *A Postmodern Reader,* ed. J. Natoli and L. Hutcheon (Albany: State University of New York Press, 1993), 427.

[5]Josiah Strong, *The New Era* (New York: Baker & Taylor, 1893), 79–80. Quoted by Sydney Ahlstrom, *A Religious History of the American People* (Garden City, N.Y.: Doubleday, 1975), 2:327.

[6]Zygmunt Bauman, *Modernity and Ambivalence* (Ithaca, N.Y.: Cornell Univ. Press, 1991), 231–45. See also J. Natoli and L. Hutcheon, eds., *A Postmodern Reader* (Albany: State University of New York Press, 1993), 10.

[7]In postmodern times, as Lyotard declares, "science, far from obscuring the problem of its legitimacy, cannot avoid raising it with all of its implications, which are no less sociopolitical than epistemological." (Natoli and Hutcheon, *Postmodern Reader,* 74).

[8]Jean-François Lyotard, *La condition postmoderne: Rapport sur le savoir* (Paris: Editions de Minuit, 1979), 7.

[9]Irenaeus, *Adv. haer.* 1. *praef.* (Alexander Roberts and James Donaldson, eds., *The Ante-Nicene Fathers* [Peabody, Mass.: Hendrickson Publishers, 1994], 1:315): "Error, indeed, is never set forth in its naked deformity, lest, being thus exposed, it should at

once be detected. But it is craftily decked out in an attractive dress, so as, by its outward form, to make it appear to the inexperienced (ridiculous as the expression may seem) more true than the truth itself."

[10]David Tracy, who clearly recognized the shortcomings of modernity, also reminds us of its benefits: "The famous 'turn to the subject' of modernity can now be seen as both emancipatory and entrapping...All of us who speak an emancipatory, liberating language are modern at heart...As are all of us who will always remain, in our lives as much as in our thoughts, believers in the democratic ideals of liberty and equality," in Tracy, "Theology and the Many Faces of Postmodernity," *Theology Today* 51, no. 1 (1994): 104–5.

Chapter 5: Mapping a New Catholicity

[1]Aristotle, *Politics* 1.2.

[2]To be found in J. Bernays, *Theophrastos' Schrift über die Frömigkeit: Ein Beitrag zur Religionsgeschichte, mit Kritischen und erklärenden Bemerkungen zu Porphyrios' Schrift über Enthaltsmakeit* (Berlin: Wilhelm Hertz, 1866), 97.

[3]Quoted in Strabo, *Geog.* 1.66.

[4]Moses Hadas, *Hellenistic Culture: Fusion and Diffusion* (Morningside Heights, N.Y.: Columbia University Press, 1959), 28.

[5]Ibid., 30.

[6]Samuel K. Eddy, *The King Is Dead: Studies in the Near Eastern Resistance to Hellenism, 334-31 B.C.* (Lincoln: University of Nebraska Press, 1961), 333.

[7]Hans Jonas, *The Gnostic Religion: The Message of the Alien God and the Beginnings of Christianity* (Boston: Beacon Press, 1958), 18.

[8]Kenneth Scott Latourette, *A History of the Expansion of Christianity*, vol. 4, *The Great Century in Europe and the United States of America, A.D. 1800 - A.D. 1914* (New York and London: Harper & Brothers, 1941), 14.

[9]John Henry Heidegger, *Medulla theologiae christianae* (Zürich, 1696), quoted in Heinrich Heppe, *Reformed Dogmatics, Set Out and Illustrated from the Sources* (London: George Allen & Unwin Ltd., 1950), 664.

[10]I have explored this subject in greater detail, and with reference to the early use of the term specifically by Ignatius and Irenaeus, in *Out of Every Tribe and Nation: Christian Theology at the Ethnic Roundtable* (Nashville: Abingdon Press, 1992), 18–23.

[11]Irenaeus, *Adv. haer.* 3.11.8-9.

[12]Tertullian, *De praes. haer.* 30.

[13]Ibid., 36.

[14]Cyprian, *De unit. eccl.* 5: *Episcopatus unus est, cujus a singulis in solidum pars tenetur.*

[15]Cyprian, *Con. Carth. sub Cyp. vii, proemium.*

[16]On this point, it may be well to note the classical division of theology, which serves to remind us of the provisional nature of any theological enterprise in this life. According to that division, there is a *theologia archetypa,* which is God's knowledge of God's self, and a *theologia ectypa,* which is all that the creature can ever attain. The latter is further divided between a *theologia beatorum,* reserved for the redeemed in heaven, and a *theologia viatorum,* which is all that we can achieve in this life. The very characterization of such theology as *viatorum* underscores its provisionality.

[17]Thomas F. Stransky, C.S.P., "The Declaration on Non-Christian Religions," in *Vatican II: An Interfaith Appraisal,* ed. John H. Miller (Notre Dame, Ind.: University of Notre Dame Press, 1966), 337.

Chapter 6: The Struggle over the History of Israel

[1]This is not to say that the God of Israel is not also the God of all nature. Unfortunately, the supposed contrast between a religion of history and a religion of nature has been used for purposes of class distinction and the oppression of the underprivileged. On this point, see chapter 2, as well as chapter 10.

²On this point, see a more extensive discussion in chapter 10.

³The text in 1 Corinthians 14:34, ordering women to be silent, is what scholars call a "floating text," that is, a text that appears in different places in the various manuscripts. Apparently this was originally a marginal note by a copyist, brought in from the pastoral epistles and later inserted in the text of Corinthians at various places by different copyists.

Chapter 7: The Struggle over Greco-Roman History

¹Justin Martyr, *I Apol.* 46.3.

²*II Apol.* 10.3.

³*II Apol.* 10.1.

⁴*I Apol.* 55.3

⁵K. Heussi, quoted by Argimiro Velasco Delgado in his introduction to Eusebius' *Historia eclesiástica* (Madrid: B.A.C., 1973), 37.

⁶Quote from personal conversations, as well as from a series of lectures delivered at Columbia Theological Seminary.

⁷Eusebius, *C. H.* 4.26.8–9. Translated by Arthur Cushman McGiffert, in Philip Schaff and Henry Wace, eds., *Nicene and Post-Nicene Fathers,* 2d series (Peabody, Mass.: Hendrickson Publishers, 1994), 1:205-6.

⁸Eusebius, *C.H.* 10.9.7-9, in Schaff and Wace, *Nicene and Post-Nicene Fathers,* 1:387.

⁹Eusebius, *Orat.* 3.5., in Schaff and Wace, *Nicene and Post-Nicene Fathers,* 1:584.

¹⁰G. R. Alton, *Renaissance and Reformation, 1300-1648* (New York: Macmillan, 1963), 6.

¹¹The Barmen Declaration, May, 1934. In Clyde L. Manschreck, ed., *A History of Christianity: Readings in the History of the Church from the Reformation to the Present* (Englewood Cliffs, N.J.: Prentice-Hall, 1964), 531.

Chapter 8: The Struggle over Secular History

¹Socrates, *C.H.* 1.1. Translated by A.C. Zenos in Philip Schaff and Henry Wace, eds., *Nicene and Post Nicene Fathers,* 2d series (Peabody, Mass.: Hendrickson Publishers, 1994) 2:1.

²Theodoret, *C.H.* 1. *praef.* Translated by Blomfield Jackson in Schaff and Wace, *Nicene and Post Nicene Fathers,* 3:33.

³Beryl Smalley, *Historians in the Middle Ages* (New York: Scribner, 1974), 55.

⁴Lactantius, *Div. Inst.* 7.14. Translated by William Fletcher in Alexander Roberts and James Donaldson, eds., *The Ante-Nicene Fathers* (Peabody, Mass.: Hendrickson Publishers, 1994), 7:211. The biblical quotation is from Psalm 90:4.

⁵Pindar, *Ol.* 2.70; Virgil, *Georg.* 1.126; *Aen.* 9.569, Ovid, *Met.* 1.132; Horace, *Epod.* 16.49. Ovid, *Ep.* 4, does express a vague hope that Saturn will restore the golden age of agriculture.

⁶Origen, *De princ.* 2.3.1.

⁷Augustine, *Civ. Dei* 12.20.

⁸Tertullian, *Apol.* 40; *Ad. Nat.* 1.9.

⁹Cyprian, *Ad Dem.* 4. Translated by Ernest Wallis in Roberts and Donaldson, *The Ante-Nicene Fathers,* 1:459.

¹⁰Augustine, *De vera rel.* 26.28. Translated by J. H. S. Burleigh in *Of True Religion* (Chicago: Henry Regnery Co., 1959), 44. (Translation slightly revised in accordance with the original Latin.)

¹¹Lactantius, *Div. Inst.* 7.15.

¹²Augustine, *De Gen. ad lit.* 1.23.35–23.41.

¹³Augustine, *Civ. Dei* 15.1.1. Translated by R. W. Dyson in *Cambridge Texts in the History of Political Thought* (Cambridge: Cambridge University Press, 1958), 634.

¹⁴*Civ. Dei* 19.17 in *Cambridge Texts,* 945.

¹⁵Orosius, *Hist.* 7.41. Translated by Roy J. Deferrari in Paulus Orosius, *The Seven Books of History against the Pagans,* The Fathers of the Church, vol. 50 (Washington, D.C.: Catholic University of America Press, 1964), 358.

Chapter 9: The Struggle over the History of the Church

[1]Preserved Smith, *The Age of the Reformation* (New York: H. Holt, 1920), 585.

[2]Bernardino Llorca, S.J., in Ricardo García Villoslada, S.J., and Bernardino Llorca, S.J., *Historia de la Iglesia Católica,* vol. 3, *edad nueva* (Madrid: B.A.C., 1967), 1044–45.

[3]René Descartes, *Discourse on Method and Meditations,* trans. Laurence J. Lafleur (Indianapolis: Bobbs-Merrill, 1960), 3–4.

[4]See the summary of the positions of historians such as Henry Boynton Smith and John De Witt in James E. Bradley and Richard A. Muller, *Church History: An Introduction to Research, Reference Works, and Methods* (Grand Rapids, Mich.: William B. Eerdmans, 1955), 20–22.

[5]Adolf von Harnack, *What Is Christianity?* (New York: Harper & Brothers, 1957), 51.

[6]Ibid., 221.

[7]Ibid., 262.

[8]Ibid., 264.

[9]Ibid., 268.

Chapter 10: The Future of Church History

[1]Justo L. González, *A History of Christian Thought,* 3 vols. (Nashville: Abingdon Press, 1970–79). Original Spanish edition: 1965.

[2]Justo L. González, *The Story of Christianity,* 2 vols. (San Francisco: Harper & Row, 1984). Original Spanish edition: 1978.